The Structure and Administration of Education in American Democracy

Educational Policies Commission

*National Education Association of the United States
and the American Association of School Administrators,
1201 Sixteenth Street, Northwest, Washington, D. C.*

Acknowledgment

SINCE the Educational Policies Commission began its consideration of educational structure and administration, the work has been carried forward largely by one of its members, DR. GEORGE D. STRAYER. In the initial stages of the project, the Commission created a special subcommittee under his chairmanship. This subcommittee held two meetings at which general policies were discussed. Thereafter, the brunt of the work in writing this document was carried by Dr. Strayer without financial compensation. For this service, the members of the Commission individually and collectively take pleasure in acknowledging indebtedness to their distinguished colleague. The Commission is fortunate in numbering among its members a man superbly qualified for the task by breadth of knowledge concerning the problems of American public schools and by a long career of constructive study of the administrative procedures suitable for the conduct of a universal public school system in this democracy. The entire project has been considered by the Commission as a whole at three meetings. It was discussed, amended, and approved for publication by the Commission in April 1938.

The Educational Policies Commission

Appointed by the National Education Association of the United States
and the American Association of School Administrators

Appointed Members

ALEXANDER J. STODDARD, *Chairman*

CORNELIA S. ADAIR

LOTUS D. COFFMAN

GEORGE S. COUNTS

EDMUND E. DAY

J. B. EDMONSON

FREDERICK M. HUNTER

JOHN K. NORTON

AGNES SAMUELSON

JOHN A. SEXSON

PAYSON SMITH

GEORGE D. STRAYER

WILLIS A. SUTTON

Ex-Officio Members

WILLARD E. GIVENS

S. D. SHANKLAND

EMILY A. TARBELL

CAROLINE S. WOODRUFF

Advisory Members

J. W. STUDEBAKER

GEORGE F. ZOOK

William G. Carr, *Secretary*
1201 Sixteenth Street, N. W.
Washington, D. C.

Table of Contents

CHAPTER ONE

*The Structure and Scope
of Public Education*

"For every child a school which is safe from hazards, sanitary, properly equipped, lighted, and ventilated. For younger children nursery schools and kindergartens to supplement home care. . . .

"For every child an education which, through the discovery and development of his individual abilities, prepares him for life; and through training and vocational guidance prepares him for a living which will yield him the maximum of satisfaction. . . .

"For every child who is blind, deaf, crippled, or otherwise physically handicapped, and for the child who is mentally handicapped, such measures as will early discover and diagnose his handicap, provide care and treatment, and so train him that he may become an asset to society rather than a liability. Expenses of these services should be borne publicly where they cannot be privately met.

"For every child who is in conflict with society the right to be dealt with intelligently as society's charge, not society's outcast; with the home, the school, the church, the court and the institution when needed, shaped to return him whenever possible to the normal stream of life."

—THE CHILDREN'S CHARTER.
White House Conference on Child Health and Protection.

I

The Structure and Scope
of Public Education

THE structure of the school system in the United
States is determined in large measure by the ideal of
equality of opportunity through education. Ours is
a one-track school system. The common expectation
is that one will begin his education in the elementary
school and will progress through the common school
to the completion of his work in graduation from high
school. For those of unusual intellectual ability, the
door should be open to the opportunities provided by
institutions of higher learning.

Limited Opportunity Is Often Associated with
Inadequate Curriculum and Sparse Population

Possibly the greatest limitation of the structure as
now developed lies in the failure to adapt the curriculums of the schools to the greatly varied abilities,
interests, and vocational outlooks of the students in
attendance. Another major limitation in structure is
found in the failure to provide education on the upper
levels, particularly in sparsely populated areas. The
realization of the ideal of equality of educational
opportunity is dependent upon effectively free education and upon the organization of adequate attendance
and administrative units.

[1]

Education Should Be Made Effectively Free

Effectively free education involves, in addition to free tuition, the provision of books and educational supplies; in many cases of transportation; and in some cases of maintenance grants necessitated by the low income of the family group from which the pupil comes. American education will reach the ideal of equality of opportunity when all barriers, whether economic or social, resulting in a denial of educational opportunity are removed. It must be recognized that the total income of the people may be increased if adjustments are made to permit larger numbers of persons to prepare for and enter those callings in which artificial restrictions in the numbers receiving training now operate. Superior ability must be conserved wherever it is found. Greater stimulation to intellectual achievement and to artistic performance is needed than is now currently found in the schools.

The Distinction between Elementary and Secondary Education Is Disappearing

The American system of public education commonly provides opportunities in elementary and in high schools. The dominant characteristic of these schools is the program of general education which they offer. Some adaptation related to varying abilities is found in many elementary schools, and differentiation of curriculums is provided in all except the very smallest high schools. The old distinction between elementary and secondary education, based upon the selective character of the latter, is no longer justified. Elementary schools enroll approximately 100 per cent of the children between the ages of six and thirteen years, inclusive. Secondary schools enroll approximately 65 per cent of the children from fourteen to seventeen years of age, inclusive.

An increasing percentage of the group eighteen and nineteen years of age is enrolled in junior colleges or in the first two years of the four-year college. The time is approaching when the common school program in the United States will provide opportunities beginning with the nursery school or kindergarten and continuing through the junior college.

Special Adjustments Should Be Made throughout the School System To Care for the Handicapped

There is need for the development of more adequate adjustment, not only in terms of curriculums but also in the regime of the school, for those who are mentally or physically handicapped and for those who are socially maladjusted. The provision of the special opportunities needed for the handicapped will often require special equipment. Examples will be found in the lighting and the size of type used in reading materials for those who have defective vision, in special furniture and other apparatus for the comfort and care of crippled children, and in facilities especially adapted to the needs of children of low mentality. In the cases of these and other handicapped children, their segregation in special classes has often resulted in more efficient school service. The organization of these special opportunities should not

[3]

deny to handicapped children association with the entire group in those activities in which it is possible for them to participate successfully.

The Traditional School Organization Is Being Modified

The typical public school system in the United States provides eight years in the elementary school and four years in the high school. Beyond these units are commonly found the four-year college and the professional and graduate schools of the university offering advanced work for three or four additional years. This pattern is rapidly being modified. The common school program now extends from the nursery school and kindergarten through the junior college. Instead of the traditional organization many communities are now organizing their school system in three major units. The first includes the nursery school and kindergarten and the first six years of the common school program; the second a four-year program of continued general education; and the third a four-year unit, an important function of which is the differentiation of courses in line with the vocational outlook of the more mature boys and girls enrolled in it. During the period of transition in which we now find ourselves a great variety of organization still exists. In some communities we have the kindergarten and the first two grades organized as a primary school; in others the nursery school and kindergarten and the first six years of the common school are organized as the elementary school. Beyond this period the variations consist of three types

[4]

of organization: (1) a three-year junior high school, three-year senior high school, and two-year junior college; or (2) a six-year high school and a two-year junior college; or (3) the organization suggested above which consists of an elementary school carrying children to approximately twelve or thirteen years of age, followed by two units of four years each which complete the common school program at approximately twenty years of age.

Administrative considerations make it desirable to organize children in three major units rather than four. For the younger children, travel distance is an important factor. Even with the diminished enrollment in elementary schools we shall still need to provide more school buildings to house little children, and the units so provided will be smaller than those in which we house older children. Beyond twelve years of age the problem of travel distance is not so important. We need, however, to provide school units covering a sufficiently long period to make possible the development of the corporate life of the school. We must recognize as well that this second unit in the school system is almost wholly concerned with the provision of general education. In rural areas the consolidation of the whole common school system in a single plant has often provided a desirable as well as an economical unit of organization.

The Structure of the Elementary School Is Changing

In many local administrative areas in the United States a one- or two-year kindergarten enrolling children four and five years of age is included as a part of the elementary school. In fewer centers the nursery school, admitting children at two and a half to three years of age, has been provided for some children. It is commonly accepted that the first two years of the traditional elementary school, enrolling children six and seven years of age, are more closely related to the work of the kindergarten and nursery school than to the upper years of the elementary school. For this reason a primary or junior school, combining the nursery school, kindergarten, and first two elementary grades, has been proposed as an important unit in the educational system.

Where such organization takes place, there remains a four-year intermediate school enrolling children from eight to twelve years of age as the upper unit of the elementary school system. This form of reorganization has often taken place without the segregation of children in separate buildings. Many modern elementary school buildings have been planned to accommodate the program of the primary school on the first floor and to provide special facilities for these younger pupils. Such modification in the structure of the elementary school is to be commended. Operating as it does to eliminate much of the rigidity and formalism of the first two grades, it is in line with the findings of child psychology and with the development of a modern curriculum in the elementary school.

The Classification of Pupils Is a Major Problem in the Structure of Elementary Education

It is common practice in the United States to admit children to kindergarten or the first grade on the basis of their chronological ages. These vary in the kindergarten from four to five years of age, and for entrance to the first grade from five to seven years of age. Whatever the age of entrance, there is a tacit assumption that the work of the school will be adjusted to the needs and capacities of children at the age at which they are admitted. As a matter of practice, however, it has been common to use the first year or two of school attendance as a period for the classification of pupils. Not infrequently from 10 to 30 per cent of the children admitted in any one year have been required to repeat the whole or a part of the year's work because they failed to master the skills associated with the grade in which they had been entered.

To overcome this maladjustment, semi-annual and even quarterly reclassifications have been proposed and carried into effect in many school systems. But even where this practice is followed, studies of retardation have clearly indicated that repetition is not a satisfactory adjustment. Other studies indicate that readiness to acquire certain skills does not occur in the same chronological period for all children. These facts have led to modifications in the classification of children in the elementary school and, in many cases, to the abandonment of fixed and uniform standards of achievement as the measure of the ability of children to make progress in the school system.

*The Social Purpose of Education Should Determine
the Classification of Pupils*

Good practice indicates that it is desirable to group

together those whose physical, social, and intellectual maturity enable them to live comfortably together. Children must be organized in groups in order that teachers, equipment, and educational supplies may be provided for them. It is an established fact that there is no particular virtue in setting a fixed period for reclassification. Good practice indicates the desirability of transferring children among the many groups which may be found in a single school whenever a better adjustment can be obtained. Certain it is that in any group of children who are under the leadership of skilled teachers, great variation in achievement will be the rule. No classification on the basis of achievement in school subjects can wipe out these differences. Children will most certainly vary in their relative standing in achievement in the various school subjects in which measurements are made.

Some Segregation on the Basis of Intellectual Ability Is Desirable

Provision is commonly made for children of very low ability in special classes. This is a desirable adjustment and is made necessary both by the specialized curriculum and the special equipment needed, and by the fact that these children work together more satisfactorily if they are not grouped with children of higher mental ability.

Quite as good a case can be made for the segregation of children of very high ability. It not infrequently happens that able boys and girls find little stimulus in association with those who are distinctly less able in intelligence. Society has a tremendous stake in the

cultivation of intelligence wherever it is found. The
school has an obligation to provide opportunities for
broadening the experience of exceptionally able boys
and girls. The adjustment which enables them to enrich
their experience in practically every area which is
included in the curriculum furnishes a sound basis for
later intellectual achievement of the highest order. The
traditional practice of rewarding proficiency in school
subjects by rapid movement through the school system
is not a satisfactory adjustment either from the standpoint of the pupil or from the point of view of the needs
of society. Equally unsatisfactory is complete and
absolute segregation of these boys and girls in special
classes.

Work in Special Classes Should Be Supplemented by Activities in Which All Participate

Children enrolled in the public schools should learn
to live together. It is unfortunate if any group develops
feelings of inferiority as a result of its school experience.
There is real danger that very able children may develop
a snobbishness which will interfere with their social
efficiency. The many activities in the school program
which lend themselves to participation by all children
should form the basis for fundamental social training.

The Size of Class Is a Matter of Primary Importance

Many of the problems of classification of pupils can
be solved by reducing the size of class. In school systems

in which children are grouped in classes of from twenty to twenty-five, teachers are able to make most of the adjustments required by variations in the abilities and experiences of their pupils. Certain special handicaps can be overcome only when children are taught in very small groups, say five or six children to the group. Remedial work in reading is a good example of this need for the organization of a small group.

The elementary school population in the United States is decreasing. A very real gain would be made if, with this decrease in the number of children attending school, the number of teachers were maintained at the present level or were increased. There can be little hope of highly successful experience for children who work in large classes. The practice in the better school systems would suggest an upper limit of from thirty to thirty-five pupils.

Some Reorganization of the Upper Years of the Common School Is Desirable

The program of secondary education in the United States is unique among the countries of the world. In the earlier period of the establishment of the public school system, and indeed down to the end of the last century, secondary education served primarily as an agency to select the more able young people and to provide them with an education which met the requirements of entrance to higher educational institutions. Within the past thirty-five years, and particularly within the past twenty years, the idea of universal secondary education has been accepted. It is true that more than three million boys and girls of secondary school age are still not in school, but it is also true that all levels of intelligence are represented in the secondary school population. The major questions of policy center around the issues of (1) what general education should be provided for all of the people, and (2) what special opportunities should be provided to prepare high school pupils for their future education or for the occupations in which they will engage.

The Reorganization of Secondary Education Will Involve Major Curricular Changes

Critics of the secondary school have properly called attention to the fact that in many instances a uniform curriculum, suited only to the needs of students of superior intelligence, has been imposed upon all the pupils. Hundreds of thousands of boys and girls in American high schools are still asked to undertake work in mathematics, in foreign languages, and even in highly differentiated sciences, in which they have little interest and in which there is little expectation that they can find utility or satisfaction. For many of these boys and girls the educational experiences provided are of no practical significance or value.

On the other hand, the criticism is made that able young people go through secondary schools without ever discovering and developing the talents which they possess. Many competent young people spend their time and energy in the social life of the school and the community, in popular amusements and in activities of little value in individual growth and development or social contribution, rather than in intellectual pursuits.

*A New Type of Secondary School
Curriculum Is Being Developed*

One of the most important experiments now being conducted in American education seeks to develop a new type of secondary school curriculum. In some schools the traditional school subjects are being reorganized in terms of the interests and needs of boys and girls in modern society. Even where a complete reorganization has not been effected, larger areas of knowledge have been organized under such classifications as the social studies, languages and literature, the natural sciences and mathematics, the fine and industrial arts, and health and physical education. A result of these experiments may be greater continuity in the program of education from the elementary through the secondary school period. The emphasis will be placed upon meaningful experience rather than upon the accumulation of knowledge. The structure of the school system may not be greatly changed, but its social significance will be greatly augmented.

*The Reorganization of Secondary Education Will
Require a Continuing Occupational Survey
and Vocational Education Programs*

A further criticism of secondary education in the United States is directed to the relationship existing between school life and the work life which follows school attendance. Relatively little provision has been

[12]

made for the preparation of young people for the occupations which they will certainly enter. There are no adequate measures of the number of opportunities to be expected in each of the many vocations. It has apparently been assumed that any boy or girl, by virtue of some sort of education, can engage in any occupation. A limited program of vocational education has been developed during the past twenty years, but these opportunities have been available to only a small minority of the total secondary school population.

The wise solution of the major problems of secondary education will require much knowledge that is not now available, and in many cases revision of the policies which now prevail in the organization of these schools. A program of general education for all citizens must be defined and developed experimentally. This will undoubtedly involve changes in the secondary school curriculums in practically all aspects. There must be conducted on a nation-wide scale a continuing study of occupations and of the need for recruits in each of the many vocations.

The Reorganization of Secondary Education Will Involve the Inclusion of the Junior College as a Part of the Common School System

The first two years of college work as commonly offered in American institutions of higher education are more certainly related to the secondary school than to the higher education offered in the last two years of college. The structure of secondary education needs to be reconsidered in terms of the junior college years. It

[13]

seems altogether likely that in the years which lie ahead most young people will not find employment before their eighteenth year. Those who wish to occupy even the minor positions of leadership may find it necessary to continue their education to twenty years of age. These are factors to be considered in the further reorganization of the secondary school.

It may be advantageous to reorganize the secondary school to include a junior high school of four years and a senior or upper high school with courses of study varying in length from two to four years. Under such a plan, the first four-year period, or junior high school, would provide general education for all boys and girls until they reach sixteen or seventeen years, with little or no vocational specialization. Adjustment to individual differences among the students would be made primarily in terms of their interests, abilities, and intellectual capacities. Some children might spend much time in music or art; others might do significant work in science by virtue of their ability to command the techniques and abstractions with which science deals; still others might find deep interest in language, in literature, or in the social sciences.

Where schools are large enough to permit the forming of several groups of the same aged pupils, it might be well to offer differentiated courses for abler students in any of the fields of study. In like manner, more of concrete experience in work with materials and in demonstrations and visual presentations might be provided for those who are less able. Fundamentally, however, all would be engaged in a program of education preparing them for living and giving them that variety of experience which would contribute to their understanding of the society of which they are members and to their satisfaction in participating in its culture.

Vocational Education Should Be a Part of the Curriculum in the Later Years of the Common School

Whether or not an organization is developed as proposed above—that is, a four-year junior high school followed by a four-year senior high school—there remains the problem of adapting the later years of the secondary school to the vocational outlook of students enrolled in them. For most boys and girls, secondary education now ends at eighteen years of age. There must be organized for these pupils courses which terminate with the end of their secondary school careers, preparing them for the occupations which they will enter. If the secondary education period is extended to include the junior college years, and if it ends at approximately twenty years of age, then this specialization can be postponed somewhat longer, for at least a part of the school population.

Terminal Courses Should Be Offered for Students Whose Full-Time Education Ends at Eighteen to Twenty Years of Age

A large majority of the pupils enrolled in the senior high school as described above would complete their full-time educational programs during the period from sixteen to twenty years of age. For all of them general education is a matter of primary importance in the development of sympathetic, intelligent, and cooperative human beings. Many of them would require little vocational education since the training needed in the occupations which they will enter is best given on the job. For some of them, courses leading directly to skilled trades might terminate at the end of the second year. For others, the program might be largely vocational during the two final years of the four year course.

A good example of the type of specialization to be offered in terminal vocational courses is to be found in the curriculums now offered in business or technical institutes for junior officers of business and industry. A survey conducted in one of the larger urban communities in the United States indicated very clearly the opportunities for work for young people with this type of specialization. It is interesting to note, as well, that in one of the eastern states half of the boys entering trade schools had completed the usual four-year high school course.

Some Specialization Should Be Provided for Those
Who Are To Continue Their Education in
Higher Educational Institutions

Let us assume for the sake of illustration a four-year junior high school and a four-year senior high school. For boys and girls who have the intellectual capacity and the ambition to carry them on through college and possibly through a professional school, the senior high school will provide courses in mathematics and science, in language and literature, in the fine arts, in the social sciences, and in health, which will be fundamental to their later education. For such of these young people as have already defined their careers, some degree of specialization may be indicated. For example, a boy who by virtue of his ability and interest has some assurance that he will continue his work in science or in engineering would benefit from emphasis on physical sciences and mathematics during the senior high school period. Other boys and girls whose interests lie in music or in the graphic arts might well spend more than the ordinary amount of time in study and in creative work in the fine arts. Similar specialization might be arranged for other groups for whom there is a reasonable assurance of continued education beyond high school.

A Major Purpose of the Later Years of the Common School Should Be Education in Citizenship

Whatever the degree of specialization undertaken by those who are to complete their full-time education by the end of the four-year high school, they as well as those who are to go on to the college and university will spend a considerable part of their time in what may properly be termed "general education." All of them should be given opportunities leading to a better understanding of the social, economic, and governmental problems which confront all members of society. All of them should find in this part of their school careers opportunities for developing interests lying outside of their immediate vocational objective, which may be developed into worthwhile recreational activities. In every case they should participate in activities for which all members of the school are eligible and in which they

[17]

may develop the spirit and practice of successful cooperative endeavor. Among such experiences might be those associated with play production, with music in all its forms, with the interpretation and appreciation of literature, with creative work in the fine and industrial arts, and with the general social life of the school community in which they live and work.

Certain Aspects of Vocational Education Should Be Considered a Part of General Education

Vocational education should be thought of as an integral part of the program made available for young people. There is no good reason why in its administration this phase of educational opportunity should be separated from general education. Only in the later years of the secondary school, students working in certain phases of vocational education may need to be segregated because of the specialized equipment required and because of the relationships which should be established between the school and industry.

For young people up to seventeen and eighteen years of age, however, it may be proposed that those opportunities which have often been called vocational should be made equally available to those who are to continue their general education and to those who may enter terminal courses leading to a particular and limited vocation. The complete separation of vocational education from general education as now organized is not justified.

The essential unity of human life and its activities suggests the desirability of developing vocational education along with all other aspects of education. The unity of the educational program should not be destroyed by the domination of a program adapted to only one of the needs of those enrolled in the schools. The goal of the curriculum and of the program of general education should be a highly unified, socially constructive, and significant educational experience for every boy and girl.

Needed modifications in the programs of secondary schools in line with this goal are already being made. Administrators and teachers recognize the importance of consolidating all educational opportunities. In anticipation of the time when coordination between vocational and general education can be achieved, every effort should be exerted by leaders in the schools to broaden the outlook and expand the objectives of secondary education so as to provide a more adequate program to meet the needs of all the pupils.

The separation of the vocational school from the ordinary type of secondary school is unfortunate. Regulations and statutes must be modified to bring about their consolidation. When these changes are brought to pass, active cooperation may be expected among groups of teachers and administrators where there is now little more than tolerance and at times open antagonism.

Special Institutions Are Offering Programs of Vocational Education

The failure of the secondary school to provide for certain types of boys and girls has resulted in the multiplication of state as well as private institutions set up to meet special youth needs. These institutions, designed to care for court assignments, unfortunates from broken homes, and the educationally and socially maladjusted, have attempted to provide satisfactory social environments and to give vocational training beyond that which public schools themselves offer. These institutions may be considered as an unplanned extension of public education, but future needs will require a clarification of the services they are expected to render and integration of these institutions in the complete educational program of the democracy.

Vocational Courses May Give Meaning to Other Phases of the Curriculum

For many students vocational studies offer the keys of enthusiasm and zeal to open the doors to educational experiences that might otherwise not have interested them. Vocational education is for some pupils an instrument for reaching the social objectives of the other more conventional school subjects. The tools of inquiry, preparation for home and citizenship, the application of science and mathematics, practical economics—all of these and many other fields, when approached from the viewpoint of the prospective vocation, often take on richer meanings to students who specialize in particular vocational offerings. Awareness of the relationships and significance of his vocation and an acquaintance with other enriching fields, tend to give the student added satisfaction in his school work and may lead to a greater degree of happiness and success in the later work of life.

Higher Education Should Be Based upon Adequate
Provisions in the Common School

The program of education beyond the upper secondary school is passing through a period of transition. It seems reasonably certain that with secondary school work eliminated from college and university, serious scholarly work will be undertaken by students in these institutions in anticipation of later specialization in professional schools or in research. It may be possible for students to complete the work of the professional schools of medicine and law in a year or two less time than is now required. Another result may be the up-grading of professional preparation for those who at present complete their education at the end of the four-year college course. Surely it would not be too much to expect that the professional education of teachers may be extended over a period of three years following graduation from the junior college.

Reorganization Is Needed in Institutions
of Higher Education

The organization of a system of higher education within the several states and within the nation as a whole presents other considerations. All too frequently the number of institutions of higher education organized by the state has militated against the development of their efficiency. In most of the state-wide surveys of higher education, recommendations have been made with respect to the consolidation of these institutions and to the allocation of functions among them. The larger issue of the development of regional institutions has also been raised. One of the most common mistakes made in this area has been the multiplication of teacher-training institutions. In some cases normal schools were originally regional secondary schools with a minimum of professional training added to the secondary school course. Once located, there has been a strong tendency to continue these institutions in service. The result has all too often been normal schools or teachers colleges with inadequate staffs, frequently poorly paid, with poor equipment, and sometimes without a sufficient population in the immediate vicinity to provide pupils for a practice school.

The determination of the program of higher education and its administration are matters deserving special inquiry. Many surveys have been made which suggest the need for reorganization in this area. It is not the purpose of this report to deal with these issues. For our purposes it is sufficient to note that the system of higher education should be developed as an integral part of the system of public education.

Independent Non-Tax-Supported Schools Form an Important Part of the Structure of Education in the United States

Paralleling the system of public schools at all levels is a system of independent and privately supported schools, colleges, and universities. The tax-supported structure does not now satisfy the need for education in the United States. This is particularly true in the field of higher education whether in colleges of liberal arts, in professional schools, or in graduate schools of research.

The independent schools in the United States on the elementary and secondary school levels are organized under church auspices or are supported by endowments or student fees. Insofar as the non-tax-supported schools are conducted on an experimental basis, they may contribute to the advancement of educational theory and practice. If they are organized on a proprietary basis and are run for profit, they have no place in our system of education. If they are supported by endowments and by student fees and are organized and administered by religious bodies or by boards of trustees, they are under obligation to provide that education which the state deems necessary for its citizens. In any event, they should be subject to general supervision by the state authority.

Adult Education Should Be Developed as an Integral Part of the Public School System

Education cannot be regarded as completed with the preparation for vocations, whether at the close of the secondary school period or at the completion of a professional course in a higher educational institution. Whether viewed from the standpoint of social need or of individual development, education is a process which continues through adult life. The development of a program of adult education is a matter of fundamental policy. The opportunities provided must be as varied as are the social and economic needs and the intellectual interests of the total adult population.

Among the fields of specialization which have been

included in programs now under way are the following: (1) Vocational training related primarily to the need for re-training, due to technological changes; (2) vocational training for those who have been injured in industry and must change their occupations; (3) up-grading opportunities preparing adults for places of major responsibility in the occupations in which they are already engaged; (4) opportunities in the social studies dealing with those social and political problems common to all citizens; (5) opportunities in language and literature, in science, and in the fine arts, whether for their vocational significance or for the opportunity which they provide for creative use of leisure time; (6) offerings in the field of health and physical education; and (7) opportunities for the study of home life, including parent education.

The Relation of the School Service to the Services of Other Social Agencies Should Be Carefully Considered

One of the more important issues to be met in the structure and organization of public education is that of the limits within which the services of the school should operate. An extreme point of view proposes that all social services needed by children should be provided under school auspices. Those who hold this viewpoint call attention to the fact that all children are assembled under the control and supervision of the schools, making possible the contacts and inquiries upon which the services to be rendered must be based. A contrasting point of view holds that the schools shall concern themselves only with instruction and that anything which

[24]

lies outside of this realm shall be left to the other social agencies operating in the community.

Other Social Agencies Should Provide
Certain Services Needed by Children

Neither of the above extreme points of view has been found satisfactory in practice. Certain of the services which should be rendered to children are closely related to the problems which confront the families from which they come. It is probable that the feeding of children who are undernourished can better be administered by an agency concerned with the welfare of the family than by the school. The provision of food and clothing for members of the family who are not in school may be just as important as is the service rendered to school children. A thoroughgoing review of the problems of health, of employment, of recreation, and the like, for the whole family may make a vast difference in the situation for a particular school child. Another example of an important service lying outside of the range of school activities is that of medical or surgical service. The schools may properly inquire concerning the physical well-being of their pupils, but the correction of remediable defects or the medical and surgical services should lie within the province of the public health agency or the private physician, surgeon, or dentist.

The Home Has Primary Responsibility
for the Welfare of Children

Whatever adjustments may be made between the

[25]

school and the other social agencies which serve children, none of them can take the place of the home. In the early years of childhood, education is carried on primarily by the family. Children come to school at four or five years of age with the most important part of their education well under way. Their health, their social understanding and habits, the richness of their experience, and their emotional stability or lack of it—all are products of the home. Nowhere is there greater need for education than in the instruction of parents concerning their responsibilities in the education of their children. No program can be successfully carried on by schools or by the other social agencies except as the intelligent cooperation of parents is secured.

The School Should Operate within the Area in Which It Is Equipped To Offer Unique Service

The difference in function between the school and other social agencies is not difficult to state. The school regime should contribute to the welfare of all of its pupils with respect to their intellectual development, their physical and emotional health, their social well-being and competence, and their ethical appreciations and standards, in order that they may certainly be prepared to live a complete life and to participate actively in the duties and obligations of citizenship. The school and other social agencies in the community assuredly must cooperate. The other agencies have obligations that transcend the areas in which the school can operate to best advantage.

No one would propose that the school be made

responsible for the treatment of communicable diseases or for the hospitalization of those who are ill or who need surgical treatment. The control of food supply and the provision of a balanced diet are not functions of the school. The school has no special obligation to provide dental service even though it may have made the pupil and his parents aware of the need for treatment.

The School May Need To Stimulate the Organization of Other Social Agencies

Children are compelled to attend school. When teachers find it impossible to perform their functions because children come to school undernourished, socially maladjusted, physically ill, or without sufficient or appropriate clothing, they may not ignore the need for the alleviation of these distressing conditions. In the absence of other social agencies to which children may be referred for aid, one of two lines of action should be taken by the school. If possible, special agencies having to do with medical and surgical care or with relief or with the many problems that center in the social life of children in their homes and in the community, should be organized. But where these agencies do not exist or where they are ineffective, teachers and school administrators should be active in the promotion of agencies for the care and protection of the children enrolled in the schools. It may be at times that most of the social services which ordinarily should be undertaken by other agencies will have to be performed by the school. As soon as these services are made available by other agencies, however, the school should willingly give up the

[27]

responsibilities which are not inherent in the provision of a program of education.

Cooperation between Schools and Other Agencies Will Result in Adequate Service for Children

Close cooperation is desirable between the school and the agency responsible for a recreational program in the community. The school has a clear obligation to provide a generous program of recreation as a part of the regular school day. When children are not using the equipment of the school, it is sound policy to make these facilities available for young people and for adults who no longer are regularly enrolled in the schools. The program, organized out of school hours primarily for those who are no longer in regular attendance, should insofar as public school facilities are used be organized under the control and administration of the board of education. Indeed, the whole program of public recreation is so certainly a part of the educational program as to make it desirable to administer even the program of adult recreation under the auspices of the board of education.

The Schools Are Concerned in the Employment Service for Youth

One of the most difficult of the decisions yet to be made concerns the responsibility of the school in bridging the gap between formal education and initial employment. That the school should play an important part in this service to youth cannot be seriously questioned. The school possesses information about boys and girls without which no wise assignment to jobs can be made. The programs of guidance which have been developed in many school systems cannot function satisfactorily unless the experience of boys and girls in employment is observed and analyzed. Initial employment involves many difficult adjustments. For many young people a series of positions have to be tried before occupational interests become reasonably stabilized. The school needs information about all phases of the job experience of its former students. Given this information, the school staff cannot only strengthen the available placement service but can as well constantly improve the related school guidance and instructional programs.

So important are the continuing contacts between the school staff and the young people on their first jobs that much is to be said for extending the practice of giving the schools primary responsibility for junior placement service wherever this arrangement is practicable. Certainly where the school is ready to meet adequately the need for this service and no other agency is, the school should not hesitate to assume placement responsibilities if the costs can be satisfactorily met. In the long run, however, the entire undertaking will demand the whole-hearted cooperation of certain other interests—such as industrial, commercial, and financial enterprises, organized labor, and the United States Employment Service. Effective cooperation among these interests may call for considerable variation in organization and functioning from place to place. No standard set-up can as yet be wisely prescribed. At the same time it is clear that for the present, if youth are to be adequately served in the matter of securing their initial employment, the schools must exhibit initiative and leadership.

The Service of Education Extends beyond the School

It is important to define the limitation which should be accepted by other social agencies in the field of education. All attempts to improve the economic and social life of the people involve education. Any health program conducted in the community will be successful just to the degree that the people are enlightened. The security which is desired for individuals and for families is dependent upon their response to opportunities for training and for those broader aspects of education which affect their leisure time activities. All the occupations in which youth and adults are engaged, whether on a full-time basis or by way of induction into a particular calling, have their very significant educational implications. These aspects of education are to be thought of as supplementing the unique service furnished by the school.

Education, When Organized as a Part of the Relief Service, Has Often Been Weak and Ineffective

It must not be assumed that the agencies dealing with relief, with health, or with recreation can carry any significant part of the systematic program of education for which the schools are organized. During the current period of depression the relief administrations—national, state, and local—have assumed large responsibility in the field of education. In many cases their handling of the educational aspects of their work has left much to be

[30]

desired. A case in point was the selection, from among those who were destitute, of teachers for nursery schools or for schools that had been closed owing to lack of funds. Poverty, lack of employment, or need for assistance are not proper bases upon which to select teachers for the schools.

Educational Aspects of Work and Relief Programs Should Be Organized in Complete Cooperation with State and Local Educational Authorities

Work programs for youth have been organized under two national administrations. The young men enrolled in the Civilian Conservation Corps camps have had some educational opportunity provided for them under the direction of professional personnel chosen by the United States Office of Education. Local work projects under the National Youth Administration have varied greatly in the emphasis given to the educational aspects of their programs. Work projects have an educational value growing out of the enterprise in which the enrollees are engaged when this aspect of the program is conceived as a major factor in the enterprise. Since the work of the Civilian Conservation Corps camps is not thought of as a program of military training or preparation of youth for military service, the camps should be organized under civilian control and administration. A larger percentage of the time of the enrollees should be given to their educational advancement. Since the camps are often located in remote areas and since they are moved from place to place, owing to weather conditions and other reasons, the general oversight and improvement of the educational program should be developed with the full cooperation of the national Office of Education and the state education offices.

The local work projects of the National Youth Administration should be chosen primarily for their educational value to those participating. Half of the time and energy of youths whose economic well-being is provided for by this enterprise, is available for their continued education. The local school system in this case should assume responsibility for complete cooperation with the representative of the National Youth Administration in the development of this educational program.

The Establishment of National Educational Authorities Endangers State and Local Autonomy

There is real danger in the suggestion that, because of the need for relief or for a new type of educational service, a new administrative authority should be created. It is possible that under this new type of organization two systems of education may develop in the United States—one, the state and local administration responsible for those who continue in school until they are employed; and the other, a national system of education responsible for youth and for adults who are no longer enrolled in the commonly recognized units of the public school system.

The nation is committed to a decentralized system of administration and control in education. As the newer aspects of education are developed, whether in the field of vocational education for young people or

[32]

in the field of adult education, they should be consolidated with the program already existing and placed under the same control and administration.

*There Is Great Need for Reorganization of the
Units of Attendance and of Administration*

One of the greatest needs for reform in the structure of American education has to do with the units of attendance and administration. In the early days of the public school system, when the population was spread sparsely over a wide area and when formal schooling consisted primarily of the Three R's, the one-room, one-teacher school served the needs of the people. This limited educational opportunity is most inadequate for those who must live and work in our modern industrial society. With the population increasing in density as well as in total numbers, and with the building of hard-surfaced roads, there is little excuse in most parts of the United States for the maintenance of the earlier type of district school organization.

*Adequate Educational Opportunities Depend
upon Relatively Large Attendance Units*

If children are to have adequate educational opportunity, they must be brought together in relatively large numbers. Adjustment to individual needs, except upon the basis of an extravagant expenditure, depends upon the presence of a sufficient number of children in any particular group to justify these special adjustments. Even when no special provision is made in differentiated

[33]

curriculums, the education of children is dependent in no small measure upon their association with others of their approximate age group. Particularly in the period of secondary education, where some differentiation of courses is clearly desirable and where terminal courses in vocational education are a necessary part of the school program, it is next to impossible to make such provision in a small school except at an exorbitant cost.

Whatever may be said with regard to the adequacy of the educational program, certain it is that economy demands that attendance units be large enough to give to each teacher a reasonable load. Classes enrolling from five to ten children, whether in a rural one-teacher school or in a high school, are expensive to maintain.

Economy in Plant and Equipment Requires
Relatively Large Attendance Units

Except in extreme cases of difficult transportation and sparse population, the attendance unit should be developed to a size that makes possible not only the ordinary classrooms but also the special facilities required for the housing of a modern educational program. In elementary schools in most sections of the United States a gymnasium is a very important facility in relation to the physical education and health program. Even children in the lower grades may use to advantage the stage of an auditorium, or may have significant educational experiences in libraries and shops. Wherever the school building is located within a reasonable travel distance of the population that it serves, community activities should be carried on in the school building.

[34]

This may well mean the provision, for both school and community use, of art and music rooms, of a cafeteria, of an auditorium with a well-equipped stage, of a variety of shops, music rooms, and the like.

Economy and the provision of a complete program of education make it desirable to organize minimum units of attendance accommodating from 300 to 500 pupils. It will certainly be economical to develop larger units of attendance, the maximum being at least 1200 to 1500 pupils, provided the transportation distance for pupils is not so great as to increase the cost unduly or to involve health hazards.

Larger Administrative Units Are Needed To Provide Adequate Leadership and To Effect Economy

Sound policy requires that in most of the states larger units of administration be organized. The criteria which should be followed in the establishment of such units may be expressed as follows:

(1) The administrative area should be large enough to make possible the employment of competent administrative and supervisory service without adding unduly to the cost of the program. Efficient administration will require, in addition to a superintendent of schools, an assistant in charge of business affairs, a supervisor of buildings and grounds, one or more attendance officers, one or more doctors and nurses, and one or more supervisors of instruction.

(2) Every administrative area should serve a sufficient pupil population to make it possible to maintain

economically the fundamental elementary and secondary school program, together with variations or adaptations needed to care for individual differences. Researches dealing with the size of the administrative unit have clearly indicated that it will be necessary to develop these units to include at least 10,000 to 12,000 pupils in order to provide the essential administrative services and to develop a complete program of education at a reasonable cost per pupil.

(3) The administrative area should be large enough to make it possible to supplement locally the foundation program guaranteed by the state in such manner as to adapt the schools to local needs and to provide for experimentation and for the expansion of the program in the light of local initiative and ambition. The realization of this objective will require a relatively large tax base and a program of state support which will guarantee an acceptable program without exhausting the tax resources of the local administrative area.

(4) The administrative area should be organized with respect to attendance areas so as to provide for minimum travel distances on roads that can be used throughout the year. It is undesirable to require children to spend more than two hours a day in traveling between home and school.

(5) Wherever possible the administrative units should be related to other governmental units in such manner as to make feasible a maximum of cooperation between the schools and other social agencies.

(6) The administrative unit should, insofar as it is

possible, represent a natural social and economic unit, to the end that all members of the community may participate in the activities of the school and feel responsible for its development.

The Profession Should Address Itself to the Reform of Local School Structure

In most of the states there is need for the reorganization of local administrative areas. The members of the profession are aware of the need for the consolidation of the thousands of local areas in which ineffective schools are maintained at a cost altogether out of proportion to the service rendered. Laymen who serve on boards of education in the more fortunate and larger areas, and public-spirited citizens, particularly those who have some acquaintance with the problems of rural life, will support a carefully considered program developed by the teaching profession. The obligation to be met is that of making provision for some millions of children whose educational opportunities wait upon the accomplishment of this reform.

CHAPTER TWO

The Administration of Public
Education: Local School
Administration

"*Fortunately the foundations of effective management in public affairs, no less than in private, are well known. They have emerged universally wherever men have worked together for some common purpose, whether through the state, the church, the private association, or the commercial enterprise. They have been written into constitutions, charters, and articles of incorporation, and exist as habits of work in the daily life of all organized peoples. Stated in simple terms these canons of efficiency require the establishment of a responsible and effective chief executive as the center of energy, direction, and administrative management; the systematic organization of all activities in the hands of a qualified personnel under the direction of the chief executive; and to aid him in this, the establishment of appropriate managerial and staff agencies. There must also be provision for planning, a complete fiscal system, and means for holding the Executive accountable for his program.*"

—REPORT OF THE PRESIDENT'S
COMMITTEE ON ADMINISTRATIVE
MANAGEMENT

II

THE ADMINISTRATION OF PUBLIC EDUCATION:
LOCAL SCHOOL ADMINISTRATION

IN MOST of the states of the Union a decentralized
system of school administration has been maintained.
Any consideration of the policies governing the administration of schools must of course include the responsibility and control exercised by the state and by the
nation. The relationship existing among these three
levels of government, and the methods employed by
each, constitute the major issues of policy. Let us first
consider local school administration.

*A Well-Established Pattern Exists for Efficient
Local School Administration*

The fundamental criterion of efficiency in the
administration of schools is to be found in the provision
of educational opportunities for children and youth.
The arrangements which make for high efficiency
include freedom from partisan political control, the
services of a competent professional staff, adequate
support, satisfactory buildings and equipment, and
curriculums adapted to the needs of pupils and to the
society which the schools are organized to serve. The
best examples of high efficiency in local administration
are to be found in the cities and villages and in some
cases in schools organized on a county-wide basis.

A Decentralized Administration Promotes Active
Participation of Citizens in the Development
of Their Schools

If reorganization of attendance and administrative units is to be brought about, the general pattern which has been found most effective can be applied with only minor modifications to the reorganized rural areas. Faith in the local administration of schools is a part of the democratic tradition. It is important that all the people should feel responsible for their government. In no area is it more necessary than in the provision of public education that the thinking, desires, and ambitions of the people be made effective. It is true that the control of educational policy is exercised by persons elected to boards of education. Nevertheless, through the exercise of the franchise, the people are in the long run enabled to determine educational policy, whether it be with respect to the support of schools, their organization, or even the program developed by the professional staff.

Local School Administration Should Be Kept Separate
from Other Functions of Government

The prevailing policy in the United States has kept the local administration of schools separate from other governmental functions. This is accomplished through setting up the board of education as a separate corporation. In the majority of the cities the local board of education enjoys the right to levy taxes, to make a budget, and in every other particular to control and administer a system of public education.

The Policy of Separate School Administration
Has Been Established Legally

The legislatures of the several states, in establishing
systems of public education required by constitution,
have created or designated local units of government to
represent them in administering details. Usually special
subdivisions of the states have been created, endowed
with corporate life, and granted power to maintain and
operate public schools wholly independently of the
municipal corporations or other local governmental
units covering the same geographic areas. Less frequently legislatures have employed existing municipal
bodies as their agents for this purpose. In such cases
municipalities have been given various degrees of responsibility, ranging from complete control of educational
matters to a few routine ministerial duties.

Education Is a Function of the State

There can be no question of the legal authority of
legislative assemblies to make all usual educational
arrangements. The state's control of education is complete and the state constitutions contain practically no
express prohibitions. Only in very exceptional circumstances can such general constitutional questions as the
illegal delegation of legislative power, the violation of
the right of equal protection of the laws, or of interference with the right of local self-government, be raised
with any show of success against any legislative arrange-

[43]

ment for local administration of public education. The question is rather one of policy.

It is sound policy which designates education as a function of the state. Since education is a matter of general concern and not one which may be left safely to the complete control of local communities, the state has the right and the obligation to mandate a general program of education. It is even more important to recognize education as a function of the state in order that there may be no doubt with respect to the independence of this function from other governmental arrangements in the local area. The state may permit a great variation in the provision of other functions of government locally, but it may never safely overlook the failure to provide adequate education for all of its children.

Efficiency in Administration Has Resulted from the Separation of School and General Municipal Administration

The question has arisen as to whether it is advisable that those portions of our state educational systems which are located in cities be in a greater or a lesser degree combined with general municipal administration. The solution of this problem will be found in a realization of the unique function of education in our American democracy as developed in an earlier report of the Commission.[1] Certain city school systems have been

[1] National Education Association and Department of Superintendence, Educational Policies Commission. *The Unique Function of Education in American Democracy*. Washington, D. C.: the Commission, 1937. 129 p.

controlled in some measure by municipal authorities. It has been inevitable in such circumstances that controversies have arisen concerning the extent of such municipal power, and the division of authority between school and city officials. These contentions have sometimes gone into the courts, and four or five hundred such cases have been appealed to the highest legal tribunals. From the decisions of the courts in these cases there is available today an authoritative record which furnishes a pertinent and important illumination of the problems under consideration.

Court Decisions Have Favored Separate
School Administration

The history of litigation on the whole favors the separate administration of education. In a few instances public education has profited through its connection with municipal government, and in a few cases city officials have used their power of control to protect the best interests of education from maladministration of school authorities. In the great majority of cases, however, educational efficiency has suffered through its association with city government. Dissension and strife have almost inevitably followed in the wake of educational control by municipal authority. Where education has been placed under the control of city officials, they have tended to regard matters of public education as a municipal affair, losing sight of the fact that public education is a function of the state and that the city is its limited agent. General municipal officers tend to forget that they have no inherent power over education and

[45]

that without legislative sanction they have no more right of control over schools than school boards have over cities. Municipal charter provisions come to be regarded as superior to the general state educational law; municipal authority as superior to the right of the state. Where limited controls have been given to cities, the tendency has been to extend them, usurping authority given by the law to school authorities. A ministerial duty of levying a tax legally requested by school boards has sometimes been extended illegally to control the uses and expenditure of the funds collected. Power given to city councils to approve or disapprove total budgets has been used as a warrant to dictate the purchase of items of supplies, the selection of school sites, the planning and erection of school buildings, and the policies of employment or dismissal and the salaries of individual members of the non-professional or teaching and supervisory staffs. Mere location of public school systems within municipal boundaries, though without a legal connection with the municipalities, has led certain cities to attempt to control the powers and properties of the independent educational authorities. Throughout the history of this litigation, municipal authorities have with impressive frequency played a role of opposition to educational development; they have traditionally taken the part of restriction, curtailment, and reluctant performance of educational duty. The record shows exceedingly few instances of municipal governments taking a position of leadership in promoting the welfare of education. It is not to be wondered at, therefore, that where litigation has arisen, the courts have most frequently held that education is a function of the state and that in the local administration of schools the board of education representing the state is supreme.

The Most Critical Problem in the Separate Administration of Schools Is the Financing of Them

One of the most fundamental considerations with respect to the local administration of schools relates to the control of the financing of this governmental service. It is easy to argue that in any locality there is a limited fund available for the support of all government and that each phase of governmental service should come before a central body to make its claims and to receive that allocation of funds which can be justified in the light of the cost of all government.

The Amount of Money Available for Education Depends upon the People's Desire and Willingness to Sacrifice

It is not difficult to challenge the premises upon which the above argument rests. There is never a fixed amount of money available for the public service. The degree to which the people pool their interests and cooperate in the furnishing of goods and services which all require, is a matter for the determination of the people. There was a time when many citizens felt that it was not right to use public funds to educate other people's children. American citizens today have come a long way from that position and are willing, for the most part, to support governmental expenditures for elementary and secondary education for all of the children of the nation.

These expenditures vary from community to community not merely in terms of the resources available but quite as certainly in relation to the idealism of the adult population. If the people have full responsibility for the selection of their representatives sitting on the board of education, they may as certainly trust this board to determine the amount of money to be invested in the public schools as they trust the other fiscal authority to determine the amount of other expenditures.

Fiscal Control Is Invariably Connected with Selection of Personnel

If the personnel in the school system, both professional and non-professional, is to be maintained on a highly professional basis and without reference to party affiliation or allegiance, then the board of education must control its own finances. In most of the other divisions of municipal government it is accepted practice to use positions in the public service as instruments of political patronage. Indeed, freedom from partisan political interference in the schools is most certainly guaranteed by the fiscal independence of the board of education.

Education Is a Unique Function of Government in Our Democracy

The argument for the separation of school administration from the other functions of government is based upon the concept of the unique function of education in American democracy. The American form of government stands or falls as the people act intelligently with respect to public affairs or fail in their responsibilities as citizens. The only sound basis upon which to maintain an intelligent citizenry is through education. If the schools are subject to partisan political control, there is no assurance that a fair consideration of common social and governmental problems will be presented to children and to youth as an important part of their education. If schools become the agency through which any particular propaganda advocated by any section of the population is promulgated, then democracy is doomed.

The Fiscally Independent Board of Education May Levy a Tax or Determine Its Budget within Certain Limits

The most common practice in the United States provides that the board of education shall have the power to levy taxes in support of education. Variations from this procedure are found where the board of education is permitted to propose a budget to be met by the general fiscal authority so long as it does not exceed a certain percentage of the total revenue available, or where the board of education is limited in its expenditures to the money accruing from the levying of a particular tax rate on the taxable property within the school district. This latter practice has been fairly successful in a number of American communities. It suffers, however, from a distinct limitation. As the necessary program of education is developed, the extent of the program and its cost tend certainly to increase out of proportion to the total population, and possibly out of relation to the returns which may be expected from local property taxes. The people may be willing to devote a larger percentage of their total budget for public affairs to education. They should have opportunity to record their will in this matter. When a tax rate which once seemed sufficient proves inadequate, the people should be permitted to vote an additional tax for the program of education which they consider essential.

Fiscally Independent Boards of Education Have Not Been Extravagant

It has sometimes been proposed that the granting of fiscal independence to boards of education will result in waste and extravagance, that men and women chosen for this most important governmental service will develop such enthusiasm for the service which they represent that they will no longer give proper consideration to the resources of the people or to the other responsibilities which they must bear. This disaster, if it may be considered such, has not occurred in those cities in which the board of education enjoys fiscal independence. Indeed, a careful study of the cost of education under the two forms of control indicates that the fiscally independent boards feel their responsibility to the people as certainly as do the general fiscal authorities who determine the budget in other cities. The cities with fiscally independent boards of education do not spend more for education than is spent in cities under the other form of control. The argument for fiscal independence does not rest upon the possibility of securing more generous support. Fiscal independence is necessary in order that the board of education may discharge its responsibility to the people and in order that partisan political considerations may not enter to destroy the efficiency of the school service.

The Fiscally Dependent Board Must Waste Time and Energy Presenting Its Budget to Another Authority

There may be added to the argument for fiscal independence the desirability of relieving those who serve on boards of education from the necessity of arguing the case for education before a general fiscal body that is little interested in education and that all too frequently acts unintelligently with respect to the program proposed by the board. Continuity in the development and maintenance of the educational program is much more certainly guaranteed where the board of education has full control. In the reverse case the school program may be greatly handicapped by the whims, the eccentricities, or the political maneuvers of the members of a city, county, or other local board of estimate and apportionment.

The General Fiscal Authority, in Determining the School Budget, Assumes Responsibility for School Policies

Where the control by the general municipal fiscal authority is complete and final, the board of education is unable adequately to discharge its functions in the local governmental organization. The program of education in any community is in very significant fashion determined by the budget adopted by the board of education. If kindergartens are to be maintained as a part of the school system, provision must be made in space, in personnel, and in equipment and supplies for this service. If home economics courses are to be offered in the junior and senior high schools, it will be necessary to estimate with great care the number of pupils to be provided for, in order that specially equipped rooms and specially prepared teachers may be made available in these schools. If significant physical examinations are to be given to school children, calculations must be made with respect to the time that must be required from doctors and nurses, the space to be made available, and the supplies and equipment necessary. If music is to include opportunities for choral work, for instruction in band and orchestra, and for individual or small group instruction, estimates of cost must be developed and provision made in the budget which will enable the school administration to carry forward this part of the educational program. And so for every other service to be rendered by the school system. When the budget is determined by a general fiscal authority, the policies which prevail in the school system are also determined by this body. If the board of education is to accept responsibility for the development of the local school system, then it must have the determination and the control of its own budget.

The Board of Education Should Have Full Responsibility for All Necessary Services of the School System

It has been argued that while the board of education should in general control its budget, great advantage would accrue to the school system and to the people through the consolidation of the administration of certain of the services required by the schools and by other governmental units. Among the areas in which it is proposed to consolidate the functions of the school board with other local administration are: the keeping of accounts and records; the selection of personnel; the purchase of material, fuel, and other standard supplies; and the use of architectural and engineering services. There are sometimes added to this list the securing of legal services and the collection and disbursement of moneys. Concerning the last two of these proposals, there is nothing in the maintenance of a separate administration and fiscal independence for schools that denies the possibility of utilizing the services of the Corporation Counsel, nor is there any difficulty in the collection of all tax moneys by a single tax-collecting agency that turns over the revenues authorized for the school to the board of education. Concerning other activities, some comment is necessary.

School Accounting Has Little in Common with Other Municipal Accounting

The accounts kept in the business office of the board of education are not identical with those that should be kept by the local government in its other divisions or services. Financial accounting for schools has little or nothing in common with general municipal accounting except as all accounting is based upon certain general principles. That accounting which lies back of the school budget has to do with the organization of schools and of classes and with the payment for services and supplies which are peculiar to the school organization. No economy could be effected by consolidating the school accounts in a general accounting office. The board of education and the superintendent of schools must have constant access to these accounts in order that they may carry on an efficient administration of schools within the limits determined by the budget for the current fiscal year.

The School Personnel Must Be Chosen with Respect to Their Peculiar Responsibilities

With respect to personnel, no general Civil Service body outside the jurisdiction of the board of education should assume responsibility for the selection of the professional personnel of the school system. It has been suggested, however, that the general Civil Service body might certify clerks, custodians, and janitors to the board of education. This proposal seems on the surface somewhat more reasonable, but as a matter of fact in practice it is of the utmost importance that persons selected for service in the schools meet requirements not commonly exacted of those who work in these same general fields in other city departments. Custodians, clerks, and janitors in the school system are in constant association with children. They form a very important group in the school personnel. They must, insofar as it is possible, be imbued with the same high ideals of service as actuate the teachers and other professional employees. They should be a superior group physically, intellectually, and morally, and acceptable to the school administration. There is no evidence that selection from a list prepared by some other body would result in any certain economy. Except under a most rigid enforcement of Civil Service requirements, the spoils system will operate in the selection of the school personnel by the general municipal authority.

The Business Administration of Schools Must Be Developed in Complete Accord with the Educational Administration

If the board of education is to be responsible for the school system it must maintain an efficient business administration. In school systems of any considerable size, an assistant superintendent in charge of business affairs operates in complete cooperation with the superintendent of schools in accounting, in the purchase, storage, and distribution of supplies, in the maintenance and operation of buildings, and the like. This business executive should be competent to purchase supplies. As a matter of record, these officers have rendered this service quite as efficiently as have the ablest purchasing agents in the general local administration. It must be borne in mind that the greater part of the expenditures for materials and supplies for schools are directly related to the educational program and that only one who is entirely familiar with that program and in intimate relationship to its administration is qualified to render the services needed by the schools.

Efficient Architectural and Engineering Service for Schools Must Be Highly Specialized

There remains the question of architectural and

engineering services. Professional opinion in this area is almost unanimously in favor of the selection of architectural and engineering services when they are needed rather than the maintenance of a regular staff of architects and engineers. Architectural service for schools is highly specialized. The man who can design a fairly adequate firehouse or police station, may not be qualified to plan a school building. There are relatively few architects in the United States who are competent in the field of school architecture. The board of education, advised by its professional staff, should, and quite commonly does, employ architectural service without reference to the geographical location of the architect's office. Interference with the selection of the highest type of service available in the country will result in increased cost to the locality in the construction of buildings and in inefficiency in planning these most important structures.

Efficient Local Administration of Schools Is Best Secured When Non-Partisan Boards of Education Are Elected

Students of administration have long agreed that the people are best represented and the schools best served when the members of boards of education are selected on a non-partisan ticket, serve for relatively long, overlapping terms, and receive no remuneration for their services. In those cities in which the members of boards of education are appointed by the mayor, it has often been found that they are under pressure to serve the mayor or the party of which he is the leader. This political obligation sometimes results in rewarding members of the party with positions on the professional and other staffs of the school system. Where board members are elected on partisan tickets and feel allegiance to the political organization, a similar situation has been found to exist. The only sound policy is that which frees the members of the board of education from any allegiance except that which they owe to the whole public. Such freedom can best be assured through nomination by petition and election on a non-partisan ballot at a special school election.

Board Members Should Serve without Salary
for Relatively Long, Overlapping Terms

It has seemed wise to expect members of boards of education to serve without pay in order that those who would seek the office for the sake of the remuneration rather than to serve the people may be dissuaded from offering their services to the public. Relatively long and overlapping terms are essential in order that continuity in the program of the schools may be maintained. In those cases in which a majority of the board members are elected at a single election or within a period of two or three years, it not infrequently happens that policies are adopted only to be abandoned before they have been fully tested.

A Small Board of Education Is Desirable

Good practice requires that the board consist of from five to nine members. This restriction in number makes it possible for the board to act as a committee of the whole. In boards composed of a large number of members, the practice of reference to standing committees has prevailed and the accompanying Senatorial courtesy has resulted in the acceptance of committee action by the whole board. Quite commonly the result is that the board as a whole never gives serious consideration to those matters which should require its attention. The practice leads, as well, to log-rolling between committees with all the recourse to petty politics so commonly associated with this procedure.

The Board of Education Should Seek the Cooperation of Organized Groups in the Community

Boards of education need to be further strengthened by keeping in close touch with the people. The issues at a single election are often not of the greatest importance and they are sometimes obscured by personalities. Where the people are keenly interested in their schools they should find it possible to present their points of view before the board of education. It is an obligation of the profession to encourage the lay board of education in the practice of inviting the cooperation of organized groups throughout the community. It has been suggested that boards of education would be made more truly representative of all the people if they were elected on the basis of proportional representation. It is essential that even small minorities be given a hearing. The purpose is not that the board shall seek to satisfy every group that comes before it, but rather that it shall act with full knowledge of the constructive thought and criticism provided by the electorate. The board of education has the further obligation to support before the people the program which it has adopted. It should act to acquaint citizens with the program of education and to defend the professional staff in the exercise of its function. Board members can often carry greater conviction in the minds of their fellow citizens than will result from the presentation of the same point of view or the same argument by a member of the professional staff of the school system.

Good Administration Requires Clear Differentiation in Function between the Lay Board of Education and the Professional Staff of the Schools

Good local administration will always be dependent upon recognition of the peculiar function of the laymen who sit on the board of education in relation to the professional service provided by the administrative staff and by all professional workers in the school system. The final authority must rest with the lay board. The schools belong to the people. But just as in the case of other professional services such as health and engineering, so in the case of education the lay board must be governed in its action by the recommendations which come from the profession.

The most important single duty performed by any board of education is the selection of its chief executive officer. Its second most important task is to hold him responsible for the program which he and it have worked out together. When this relationship exists, the members of a board of education do not act as "rubber stamps." They require that the superintendent of schools and his associates bring before them for consideration a program which can be justified in terms of educational theory and which can be financed from the resources which are available. Good members of a board of education scrutinize carefully each proposal brought before them by the superintendent of schools. They constantly require that their executive officer present proof of the wisdom of the measures which he has advocated and that he give a strict accounting of his use of the resources provided.

The Relationship between the Board of Education and Its Executive Officer Needs To Be Defined

In order that the relationship between the board of education and the superintendent of schools may be acknowledged by both parties, it is necessary that the board adopt rules of procedure which will be modified only for reasons of great weight. Among the rules now commonly in operation in school systems that are efficiently operated, are the following.

The Superintendent of Schools Should Nominate All Employees and the Board of Education Should Elect Only upon His Nomination

The board of education requires its chief executive officer, the superintendent of schools, to nominate all associate or assistant superintendents, supervisors, directors, principals, teachers, and other professional employees, and all non-professional employees. The board of education fills positions that are vacant only upon the nomination of the superintendent of schools. This rule seeks to center responsibility in a single executive officer. It is opposed to the idea of a coordinate executive officer called the business manager or business superintendent. It requires that however certainly the superintendent may delegate responsibility, nevertheless all recommendations clear through his office, and in the last analysis he assumes final responsibility for the efficiency of the whole staff.

Matters of Curriculum, Processes of Teaching, Materials and Supplies, and Organization of Schools and Classes Should Originate with the Superintendent of Schools and His Staff

The board of education provides that in all strictly professional matters, such as the adoption of textbooks or the development of courses of study and curriculums, recommendations come before it from the superintendent of schools. The board may by rule propose the measures to be taken in securing the cooperation of other members of the professional staff in the development of these recommendations. Boards of education have in some cases wisely established departments or divisions of the supervisory and administrative staff dealing with certain of these more important professional problems. But whatever the arrangements may be with respect to the utilization of staff, it is important that the board recognize the responsibility of that staff and that it does not take upon itself a duty or a responsibility that can be exercised only by those who are professionally competent.

[61]

The Board of Education Should
Hold the Superintendent of Schools
Strictly Accountable for Results

The board of education requires that the superintendent of schools keep it informed with respect to the achievements and progress that are being made in the school system. These reports may take many forms. At one time the issue may deal primarily with the adaptation of curricular offerings to the needs and capacities of children. At another time problems of reorganization of the attendance units within the school system may be matters of major importance. At still another time the recruiting, assignment, salaries, tenure, and retirement of teachers may properly engage the attention of the board. Again, the relation of the schools to the community and the significance of the curricular offerings as measured by their relationship to modern social life may be expounded by the professional staff for the benefit of the laymen sitting on the board of education. And so for any other major problem confronting the schools.

The Superintendent of Schools Should
Submit an Annual Budget for the
Consideration of the Board of Education

The board of education requires the superintendent of schools annually to submit a budget, together with the program of work to be accomplished and the estimated costs by divisions and activities of the school system. These budgetary estimates should be based upon analyses of costs in previous years by divisions of the school system and by units of the school organization. Budgetary estimates should always include a salary schedule based upon principles which can be applied uniformly throughout the school system. No budget would be complete without an estimate dealing with the need for capital outlay and for the maintenance and operation of plant and equipment. The superintendent of schools may not be a budgetary expert, but certainly he and his associates are in much better position to furnish sound information with regard to the needs of the school system for support than are even the ablest business men who sit on the board. In a school system that is well staffed the superintendent will have as one of his associates a man specially trained in the business practices of the school system, upon whom he can place large dependence in the development of the budget.

The Superintendent of Schools Should Study
Plant and Equipment Needs and Present
the Capital Outlay Budget

The board of education requires the superintendent of schools to keep it fully informed with respect to the need for new sites and new buildings. In a school system of any considerable size shifts in population and the increase or decrease in school attendance that may be expected over a period of years involve major problems of the size and location of school buildings. It is as feasible to proceed scientifically with respect to the development of a capital outlay budget as it is to

[63]

conduct any other business enterprise on the basis of carefully considered facts. After studies have been made with respect to the need for plant and equipment, estimates should be submitted concerning the financing of such additions to the plant as may be necessary or expedient.

Administrative Details Should Always Be
Left to the Professional Executive

The board of education should not concern itself with the details of administration in the operation of the schools. If board members have confidence in their professional staff, they can very well leave all except the major issues to the determination of the superintendent of schools and his associates. Possibly the soundest procedure is found in the adoption of those rules that have the most general application, leaving their interpretation to the profession. Certainly nothing can be more foolish than for a board of education to allow itself to be maneuvered into a position where it must treat each case arising in the school system with respect to such details as the placement of children in particular schools, the assignment of teachers, or the granting of permission to recognized groups for the use of buildings and grounds.

The Board of Education Should Act
as a Committee of the Whole. There
Should Be No Standing Committees

In the conduct of its business the board of education

acts as a committee of the whole. There may be exceptional cases where a temporary special committee may investigate a particular field, but even when this is done the report should be made to the committee of the whole and the issues, whatever they are, should be considered by all members of the board. As has been suggested above, when boards of education are organized into many standing committees—usually as many committees as there are board members—the overwhelming tendency is to deny to the board as a whole the consideration of even the major issues which should be brought before it. Men and women who are competent to sit upon boards of education should not find themselves in a position where they must give their time and thought to a problem in a committee and then repeat the process again before the whole board.

Able members of boards of education should give their best thought to the major issues which confront the school system. They should be guided but not controlled by their professional executive and members of his staff. They should require evidence in support of any position they are asked to take. They should constantly check against the action of their staff and the policies which they have approved. It is only when the board of education operates after this fashion that it can serve the public.

Efficient Administration Requires the
Organization of a Staff with a Clearly
Defined Line of Responsibility

Good administration requires the organization of the

staff of the school system in relation to the specialized functions which they serve. There can be only one responsible executive. If the school system is large, he must have associated with him persons in whom he can place confidence and to whom he can give responsibility. They in turn must carry out in the school system the program which has been adopted, through the offices of the principals of the several schools and in the actual work in the classroom.

It is futile to propose that members of the professional staff of the school system can work as individuals without accepting responsibility on the one hand and giving loyal service on the other. There is nothing in such a relationship which need deny to any individual the exercise of freedom of thought and the attempt to carry forward his part of the program in an intelligent fashion. To propose that there is no line of responsibility is to propose anarchy.

The Entire Staff of the School System Should Take Part in the Formulation of the Educational Program

In all that is proposed with respect to the administration of schools, there is implicit an acknowledgment of the contribution to be made by the educational profession. To indicate the place of leadership in all good administration is not to deny the large part to be played in the development of policy by all professional workers. Our schools are organized for the purpose of educating children, young people, and adults for participation in democratic society. Any significant realization of this purpose will require independent thinking, a large degree

[66]

of cooperative endeavor, and broad sympathy and understanding on the part of all who are enrolled in educational institutions. Certainly these virtues may not be expected to abound among those who are taught unless they are found also in the experience of teachers. Surely in no area may teachers more certainly exercise independence of thought, cooperation in action, and social understanding than in their daily professional work. It is sound procedure to provide for the active participation of teachers in the development of administrative policy.

Teachers Have a Right and an Obligation To Contribute to the Development of Educational Policy

The formulation of school policy should be a cooperative process capitalizing the intellectual resources of the whole school staff. This participation in the development of educational policy should not be thought of as a favor granted by the administration but rather as a right and an obligation. Some plan should be provided through which the constructive thinking of all the workers in a school system may be utilized. After policies have been developed by the staff they should be submitted to the board of education for final review and approval. When approved, every member of the school system for whom it has implications becomes responsible for carrying into effect the adopted policy. This procedure promotes efficiency through individual understanding of policies and through the acceptance of joint responsibility for carrying them into effect. What is far more important, it provides a democratic process through which growth in service is promoted and the school service itself profits from the application of heightened morale and of group thinking to school problems. It makes the school in reality a unit of democracy in its task of preparing citizens for our democratic society.

The Schools Should Seek the Cooperation of Laymen

Schools should be organized in relation to the immediate community from which the children come in the interest of the larger local community and in the service of the state and nation. Citizens have an obligation to cooperate with the school in the education of children. All too frequently schools have existed in almost complete isolation from the communities which they seek to serve. They have commonly made little or no provision for utilizing the resources—economic, social, and personal—which immediately surround them. In ideal school and community relationship the school seeks the cooperation of parents and other citizens in developing its program. It must, as well, utilize the experiences of children in the community and take them out of the school environment into the varied community environment for many experiences which cannot otherwise be made available.

Staff Officers May Contribute Significantly to the Development and Improvement of the School Service

Whatever may be the organization of the administrative staff, there remain other services which should be furnished from the central office by persons who are usually called staff officers. These are they who, having high competence in some special field, are placed in the school system where they can serve the other members of the staff. A splendid illustration of this type of relationship is the position held by a good supervisory officer. The good supervisor has ideas based on research and on successful professional experience. These ideas may be made available through demonstration or discussion to teachers and to other professional workers. The essential quality of good supervision is found in the high competence of the supervisor and his willingness to work in cooperation with the teachers with whom he is associated. It is only when teachers feel entirely free to express their own ideas and equally free to reject those which in their judgment are of less worth, that the relationship of supervisor to teacher may be expected to result in professional growth for those who are supervised.

Other staff workers occupy similar positions in relation to administrative officers and to teachers. The service of the director of research may be of very great importance to the superintendent of schools. A scientific inquiry conducted by this staff officer may make possible the successful modification of practices carried on in the classroom. All other staff officers hold similarly important positions. Those who are responsible for attendance and other social services aid teachers, principals, and administrative officers. The health service is closely related to the welfare of every child in the school system, and conditions the work of all the professional personnel. The business office should be thought of as a staff office since it exists not for the sake of conducting business transactions but rather for the sake of providing those conditions in plant and its maintenance and operation, in supplies and books, in the handling of the payroll, and in all other financial transactions, which make it possible to operate an efficient school system. It is good administration to distinguish between the line of responsibility exercised by those who carry the educational program through to a successful conclusion and the function of those who enter the situation at the request of administrative officers, teachers, or other employees to render the special service which they have to offer.

School Principals Are
Important Line Officers

Good administration places large responsibility in the hands of the principal of the school. However a school system may be organized, the unit which means most to children and to their parents and the community at large is the individual school unit. It is only when those placed in charge of these several units within the school system recognize the importance of their work and carry large responsibility for its development that the best results can be secured. Good administrators have from time immemorial recognized the necessity of modifying the program adopted for the school system as a whole to fit the needs of a particular locality and to fit into the particular point of view that is developed by a principal and a group of teachers. Nothing can more certainly interfere with the growth of teachers and the significant education of children than administrative action which seeks uniformity in organization and in procedure in all schools throughout the system.

Uniformity of Practice within a School System or a
Single School Is neither Necessary nor Desirable

In like manner, within a single school good administration requires that the principal protect the teachers against a policy of too great uniformity. It is always possible to develop a program following a general scheme or pattern while allowing to individual teachers a large degree of freedom. The skillful principal discovers special aptitudes and abilities wherever they exist in his teaching staff and encourages those variations in practice which are the peculiar genius of the individual teacher.

Local School Administration Is of
Surpassing Importance in Our Democracy

If the schools are to serve the democracy, they must be kept in close touch with the people locally. Whatever the general program that may be mandated by the state, the schools will fail of their purpose unless they reflect the interests, the ideals, and the devotion of the community which they serve. It is reasonable to propose that local school systems be adjusted to the peculiar needs of the local area. It is essential that the professional staff of the school system be supported in its work by the participation of intelligent citizens in the development of curriculums and in the provision of experiences outside of the school for the children enrolled. In order that the schools may most certainly represent the people, it is important that the people choose their representa-

[71]

tives for places on the board of education without reference to partisan politics. It is essential that those who are so chosen keep closely in contact with the public which they serve and with the professional staff which they employ. Only on the basis of complete and whole-hearted cooperation among the professional staff of the school system, members of the board of education, and the community at large, can education effectively serve our democracy.

CHAPTER THREE

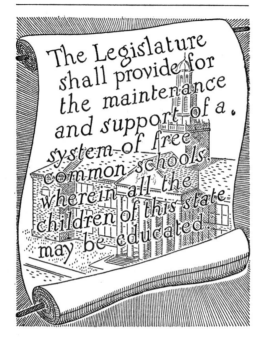

*The Administration of Public
Education: State School
Administration*

"The legislature shall provide for the maintenance and support of a system of free common schools, wherein all the children of this state may be educated."
—NEW YORK STATE CONSTITUTION,
Article 9, Section 1.

"The state should insure equal educational facilities to every child within its borders at a uniform effort throughout the state in terms of the burden of taxation; the tax burden of education should throughout the state be uniform in relation to tax-paying ability, and the provision for schools should be uniform in relation to the educable population desiring education. Most of the supporters of this proposition, however, would not preclude any particular community from offering at its own expense a particularly rich and costly educational program. They would insist that there be an adequate minimum offered everywhere, the expense of which should be considered a prior claim on the state's economic resources."
—GEORGE D. STRAYER AND ROBERT M.
HAIG, THE FINANCING OF EDUCATION
IN THE STATE OF NEW YORK

III

THE ADMINISTRATION OF PUBLIC EDUCATION:
STATE SCHOOL ADMINISTRATION

THE responsibility for the provision of public education in the United States rests primarily with the
several states. The constitutions of most of the states
require that the legislature establish a system of free
public schools open to all of the children of the state.
Under this mandate, the legislature determines the form
of organization and control of the public school system.

Quite commonly large responsibility for the support
of education and for the determination of the program
has been left to local units of control and administration.
Local boards of education are the instruments used by
the state for the performance of its function. This
relationship has been clearly indicated by Constitutional
provision, by legislative enactment, and by decisions of
the courts. In delegating responsibility to the local
administrative area, the state does not relinquish all
responsibility or authority over the public school system.
On the contrary, state boards of education with well-
defined powers and state superintendents or commissioners of education having considerable administrative
responsibility are provided in each of the states.

*The Administration of the Schools Should
Be Kept Close to the People*

It is of great significance that the people have insisted
upon the control of their affairs locally. Local organiza-

tions inherited from the days of limited possibilities of transportation and communication may need to be revised. It will often be necessary, in the interests of efficiency and economy, greatly to enlarge the unit of administration, but the size of the unit should not be determined solely by the efficiency with which the job can be done. There are the more fundamental considerations of the feeling of responsibility and the prob ability of participation by people locally which may outweigh the consideration of maximum efficiency. Schools more than any other function of government are of surpassing interest to the people. It could not be otherwise, for all normal human beings are interested above everything else in their children and in their future. It is the normal ambition of adults in any community to provide education for their children superior to that which they themselves enjoyed. They seek through education to provide better lives for their children and a better society in which the oncoming generation may live and work.

The Local Control and Administration of Education Is the School of Democracy

In a democracy the people should feel their power to modify the situation in all areas of government. All too frequently in matters that come before state and national legislatures, the great majority of people feel that they have little to contribute and that they lack power of action. Even in the organized pressure groups that seek to influence state and national legislation, most of the adherents feel that it is the organization's officers or lobbyists who determine matters for them. Citizens frequently subscribe to programs of action to which they have given little consideration.

If all citizens are to participate intelligently in all phases of government, it must be on the basis of intelligent interest in those affairs which are near at hand. Only gradually may the intelligent citizen be expected to move from the consideration of his local government to an understanding of and an active participation in the affairs of those other governments that are more remote.

Centralized Administration of Education
Is Likely to Result in Mediocrity and
in Lack of Local Adaptability

Centralization in the control, administration, and financing of education is very apt to lead to a mediocre school system and a lack of progressive development of the program of public education. With well-developed local units for the administration of schools, it is certain that some communities will develop leadership which will be effective in improving education. It is in these areas, in which experimentation occurs and in which the high idealism leads the people to sacrifice for the maintenance of an adequate system of education, that demonstrations will be made which may later affect the whole program of education throughout a state or even throughout the nation. Most of the great reforms in education have originated in the schools of some local community; they were not decreed by a central authority.

*Educators Should Distinguish between Legislative
Action Which Promotes Educational Progress
and That Which Is Inimical to It*

A particularly vicious form of centralization in the
control of education is found in legislation dealing with
specific aspects of the curriculum. The state undoubtedly has the right and the responsibility to mandate
a system of public education and to require that all of
its citizens be subjected to the educative process. It
may without interference with local initiative and responsibility indicate in broad outline the program of
education to be offered in the common schools. The
general scope of the common school curriculum may be
indicated without denying to the profession and to
local communities the privilege of adapting this general
program to their local needs. It is reasonable to require
that schools everywhere give attention to language and
literature, to science and mathematics, to the social
sciences, and to the fine and industrial arts. It is proper
that education shall contribute to the physical well-being
of boys and girls. No one would seriously doubt the wisdom of imposing upon local communities the requirement of a school term of one hundred and eighty days
or more. It is necessary that the state outline the conditions under which local units of administration may
be organized. It will probably be necessary, as well,
that authority be vested in the central office to effect
reorganizations where manifest inefficiency and a lack
of educational opportunity result from an ineffective
organization.

The Development of Curriculums and of Teaching
Processes Should Be the Duty of the Professional Staff

In contrast with these areas in which the state or
other central authority may operate with advantage
to all concerned, is the field represented by the curriculum of the schools and the teaching process. In the first
place, the development of curriculums and of programs
of activities to be carried on in the classroom is essentially
a professional matter. No legislative body is competent
to deal with the problems that arise in these areas. It
would be as safe to legislate with respect to technical
matters involved in the construction of a bridge or the
routine to be followed in a hospital as it is to legislate
with respect to the details of the curriculum or the
methods to be employed in the classroom. The issue
raised is not academic. Members of the profession and
friends of the public school should stand fast against
well-meaning groups who seek legislation in support of
their particular interests in the education of children.
However worthy their programs may appear to be,
they can be acceptable to the schools only on the basis
of their development in relation to the total program.

Piecemeal legislation requiring the teaching of hu-
maneness, the instruction of children in safety, the
presentation of the problems of conservation, all specifying the grade-level and time-allotment, will not secure
the ends which their proponents desire, and may result
in serious interference with the general program of education conducted locally. The suggestion is not that
the profession seek to resist changes in the curriculum
which will enrich the experiences of children or adjust

[81]

them to modern social life. The objection is against the attempt to improve the curriculum by piecemeal legislation which ignores the necessity of relating new materials to the total experience provided for children. The way for a community to keep its program of education in accord with the needs of the times is not to mandate the details of the educational program by legislation but to set up adequate machinery and competent professional service to bring the desired program into actual fulfillment.

State Boards of Education Should Be
Selected without Party Designation for
Relatively Long, Overlapping Terms

All too frequently the state board of education is an ex-officio board and for this reason may be little interested in the development of the state's program of education. In a majority of the states the state superintendent of schools is elected by popular vote. This practice militates against the securing of the highest type of professional service for this most important office. There is need for a campaign throughout the United States for the establishment of state boards of education composed of laymen whose primary interest is in the educational service, and for the selection of state superintendents or state commissioners of education by this body.

There are two current practices which have been found acceptable in the selection of members of state boards of education. In some of the states a long tradition of the selection of able and interested citizens through appointment by the Governor has been found satisfactory. In other states the election of the state board by popular vote has been undertaken without reference to political affiliation and has likewise resulted in the selection of competent citizens for this most important service. In either case the success of the method employed depends upon the interest that the public takes in the selection of the state board and their insistence that party politics shall not enter to determine the selection of the members of this body. There is the possibility of failure to provide a competent state board by either of these methods. If the Governor feels that he may serve his party by nominating to these positions of honor those who have supported him, the state board may lack competence and may actually operate in a fashion which will injure the cause of public education. If the naming of the elective board is dependent upon nominations in party caucus and if again the selection is made as a reward for party regularity the same unfortunate results will follow. Whatever the method employed, the competence will rise no higher than the interest and the vigilance with which the citizens of the state insist upon the selection of persons whose sole interest in membership on the board lies in their desire to serve the cause of public education.

Popular Election of a State Superintendent of Schools Cannot Secure the Highest Professional Competence

It is unfortunate that in so many states the chief school officer is elected by popular vote. Able men and women have been elected in this manner, but all too frequently nominations for the office have been offered to those of little professional reputation or to those who are willing to support the party program and ticket. Sometimes a contribution to the campaign fund, representing a considerable part of the salary involved, has been the price paid for the nomination. Furthermore, election by popular vote carries the implication of a relatively short term of office, usually two to four years. In some states, furthermore, the chief state school officer is not permitted to succeed himself. In many cases he may spend his energy during the larger part of the period of his service in building his fences for re-election. No state superintendent or commissioner of education can hope to carry into effect a significant program in so short a period or under such conditions.

Appointment of the State Superintendent of Schools by the Governor May Result Unfortunately

Another method of selecting the chief state school officer is appointment by the Governor. There is a possibility that the Governor will choose for this office a professional worker of high competence. There is also the very great probability that, with the overturn of a party in any election, the Governor coming into office will appoint one who is acceptable to him personally and to the party which has won the election. It has happened within recent years that men of the highest competence in the state office, who owe their appointment to the Governor, have been replaced as the result of an election which changed the political control within the state. Whatever may be the idealism or the lack of

[84]

it actuating the Governor in the appointment of a state board of education, it is reasonably certain that this body will be less likely to play politics with the office of commissioner of education than will the Governor.

State Boards of Education Have Commonly Selected Men of High Professional Qualifications for Their Chief Executive Officers

When the state board of education, appointed by the Governor or elected by popular vote, has responsibility for the choice of the state superintendent of schools or the commissioner of education, it will commonly be free to select this important official from among all qualified professional persons, without regard to place of residence or party affiliation. This is as it should be. It is common practice, as well, for the executive so selected to serve at the pleasure of the board. Thus the issue of continuance in office is not raised periodically.

The State Board of Education Should Look for Leadership to the Professional Executive and His Staff

The state board of education should enjoy the same relationship to its executive officer as is found in the practice of the better administered local school systems. The state commissioner of education should be in position to search for men and women of high professional competence and, upon his nomination, these persons should be elected by the state board of education. It cannot be expected that the best type of staff can be assembled under the politically dominated control associated with the popular election of the state superintendent of schools.

The State Board of Education Is Largely Responsible for the Development of the School System

The state board of education, acting on advice from the commissioner of education and the specialists who work in cooperation with him in the state office, exercises general oversight of the public school system of the state. It has responsibility for instigating legislation which will establish local administrative units and set the general pattern for local organization of education. It should recognize the responsibility of the citizens of each local administrative area for the development of their own school systems. The state board should be authorized by law to seek the cooperation of the citizens of local administrative areas in the determination of the boundaries of local districts. Such cooperation is most desirable in this period when there is need for transition from the early small district organization to adequate local units of administration.

The State Office of Education May Properly Be Given Control of Certain External Aspects of Education

The state authority should be exercised with respect to certain minimum requirements dealing with the external affairs of the schools. Among these *externa* are the following:

(1) The state must determine in broad outline the

scope of the educational program to be provided in local communities. The legislature may well provide that the state department of education be given power to enforce the provision of education for children in nursery schools and kindergartens, in elementary and high schools, in vocational schools, and in classes for adults, in every local unit of administration.

(2) The state may well require its department of education to enforce the compulsory attendance law for those in the age groups to which it applies.

(3) If the purpose of the state is to be realized in its schools, the minimum length of school term must be enforced.

(4) Only when the state accepts full responsibility for the certification of teachers and their tenure and retirement and pensions, will competent personnel certainly be secured.

(5) The state office should be equipped to pass judgment upon plans for school sites, school buildings and their equipment, in terms of minimum standards, providing not only for the safety and physical well-being of children but for the accommodation of the program of education which the state seeks to maintain.

(6) To determine the degree to which the state's requirements are being met, reports must be required to the central office of educational and fiscal data from all local administrative areas.

(7) To insure adequate general budgetary procedure and sound fiscal accounting procedure, the general supervision of the state office will be needed.

In no case should the state's requirements be interpreted as maximum standards. Local units of administration should be encouraged to exceed the required minimum program. The state should not enter a situation to determine the details of the curriculum or the methods to be employed in the classroom. In the internal affairs of the school system the local administrative and supervisory officers and professional workers should be given full responsibility.

Satisfactory Relationships between State
and Local Administration Depend upon the
Establishing of Larger Local Administrative Units

One of the difficulties confronted in state administration of education is the weakness of local administration outside the urban areas. It has often been argued that only as state curriculums and courses of study are provided is there any assurance that teachers locally will carry forward an adequate program of education. It is proposed that the state, in adopting a uniform system of textbooks, guarantees to children in all localities the provision of good books. It has even been suggested that the only way in which the state can be certain of the adequacy of local programs is through conducting state examinations of the pupils in the schools.

The answer to these and to similar arguments is to be found in the reorganization of local administrative areas, as proposed above. When local units of administration are large enough to provide a complete system of public education, and when these local administrative areas have sufficient financial resources to employ highly competent professional leadership, then the state need not and should not attempt to determine the details of the educational processes carried on in the local school system.

Where Adequate Local Administration Exists, the State Office Acts as a Source of Information, Leadership, and Supervision

Where local administration is competent, the primary function of the state office in dealing with the internal affairs of the schools is that of leadership. The state department of education that is well staffed should be thought of as a great service organization to which any local administrative officer or group of teachers may apply for guidance.

The state office staff should be prepared to give counsel and advice, based on the results of scientific inquiry and experimentation. They should be sufficiently well acquainted with the best work that is carried on by the various schools and school systems within the state to act as a clearing house to distribute to all members of the profession adequate reports of the best practice.

Problems dealing with the development of curriculums, with the teaching process, with the organization of schools, with the provision of books and equipment, and with the local financing of schools should be brought to the attention of specialists in the state department, with the expectation that competent advice will be forthcoming.

[89]

*The State Board of Education Should Cooperate
with the Boards Responsible for Higher Education
or for Other State Educational Institutions*

In the discussion thus far the state board of education
has been conceived as the body responsible for the maintenance of the common school system. In most states
one or more additional boards of education exist to control and administer institutions of higher education
serving the whole state. Ideally, all public education—
elementary, secondary, special, and higher—should be
under the general supervision of a single board of education, but this ideal is not likely to be generally realized
in the near future. Possibly the best adjustment that
can be hoped for is the establishment of one board of
education responsible for local school systems on the
elementary and secondary school levels, and the consolidation of all boards of education having to do with
higher education in a single body. The responsibility
sometimes allocated to special state bodies, such as text-
book commissions and state boards for the certification
of teachers, should rest with the state board of education
responsible for elementary and secondary education.
Whatever the disposition of the matter may be within
a single state, good practice requires the cooperation of
all boards of education in the development of an inclusive program of public education.

*There Is Need for Unification of the
Program for Teacher Education*

In most of the states many institutions of higher

education under public and under private control offer curriculums for the preparation of teachers. It is often true that even in the publicly supported institutions there is a lack of coordination among teachers colleges, the state agricultural college, and the state university. The lack of a unified program and the failure to estimate accurately the needs of the state for teachers have resulted in the preparation of thousands of young men and women for the teaching profession for whom there are no places in the public school system. It is only upon the basis of the development of a unified program of higher education and the allocation of functions among the several institutions that the state can use its resources to best advantage and the young people enrolled in these institutions can receive appropriate guidance in the selection of the curriculums in which they should enroll. The ultimate goal in the development of our system of public education will be reached when a unified program, including elementary, secondary, and higher education, is organized to meet the demands of our democratic society and to provide for a complete life for every individual.

The Professional Staff of Higher Institutions Should Be Given Responsibility for the Development of Curriculums. Each Institution May Develop Some Special Curriculum

As has been proposed in another section of this report, the local units—in this case, state teachers colleges—should reflect the insight, ability, and competence of the professional staff responsible for the program carried on in each separate unit. The state board of education may properly assign special functions to each of the several state teachers colleges; for example, one of these institutions might offer unusual opportunities in the field of physical education, another might offer courses for the preparation of specialists in music or art, and still another assume major responsibility for the preparation of teachers of commercial subjects. But whether or not any such special assignment is made, the success of the teacher-education program will in the last analysis rest upon the competence of the executive officers placed in charge of each of these institutions and on the financial support which will make possible the employment of highly competent professional staffs.

The State Board of Education Should Propose Legislation To Equalize the Support of Education throughout the State

In no area is the state board of education more certainly concerned than that of support. It is impossible to provide an adequate program of education in all administrative areas within the state on the basis of local taxation. It is the obligation of the state commissioner of education and of the state board of education to propose a program of state financing of schools that will guarantee a reasonably adequate educational opportunity to all the children of the state wherever they live.

The best practice in the United States seeks through the equalization of support from the state to guarantee a fundamental or foundation program of financial support of education for all children, and to equalize the burden of taxation to be borne in support of this program among the several administrative areas. To carry into effect a program which will provide for the equalization of educational opportunity will require, first of all, a definition of the program for which the state assumes responsibility. It is not enough to propose that well-qualified teachers be provided for all children or that books and other educational supplies be made available for them. Even when the definition of opportunity includes a statement with respect to buildings and equipment, curricular offerings, length of the school term, provision for health and for educational and vocational guidance, and the like, the real problem may still be unsolved.

In the last analysis, if opportunities are to be equalized up to any given level, the best definition of this level will probably be found in the current cost of education in communities of average wealth. In those areas in which transportation must be provided, this cost will need to be added.

State Support Should Be Based on Measures of Educational Need and of Financial Ability in Each Local Administrative Area

Having established the cost of the program which the state will guarantee, there remain two major considerations—one, what is the need of the local administrative area for support; and two, what is the ability of each local community to provide the funds necessary for the maintenance of its schools?

A rough measure of the need for support may be

found in determining the number of classroom units to be supported. This will be relatively simple in the larger schools where multiples of an acceptable class size are used as a measure of the need in elementary and high schools. Wherever small attendance units are maintained, a correction will have to be made which will guarantee a minimum number of teachers for each of these attendance units.

Possibly the simplest measure of the ability of a community to support its school system is found in the application of a common tax rate to equalized assessments of property throughout the state. When a formula involving these factors has been developed, it will be found in every state that the ability of local areas in relation to their need will vary greatly. In one case the proposed tax rate may yield as little as 20 per cent of the cost of the equalized program that the state seeks to maintain. In another case the application of the same tax rate may provide as much as 90 per cent of the cost of the foundation program. In the first case the state will be called upon to supplement local resources by 80 per cent of the cost of the minimum program. In the other case state funds would provide only 10 per cent of the cost of the foundation program.

The State Should Encourage Local Administrative Units To Exceed the Fundamental Program Guaranteed

Wherever state support is given to equalize educational opportunity and the burden of support, there should be the expectation that many localities will develop their programs beyond the standard required by the state. For this reason any tax rate used as a basis for calculating local ability should be a relatively low rate. The people locally should be in position, without undue sacrifice, to add to the state's mandated program in such measure as is in their judgment desirable.

Only when freedom to exceed the state program is granted, may those variations in the educational program be expected which will make for progress. After a period of years, and certainly by the time that a majority of the communities have exceeded the state's fundamental program, it is reasonable to expect that the state will raise the level of its foundation program. The initiative exercised by local communities will in the long run contribute to the elevation of the standard of educational opportunity provided in all schools of the state.

The State Education Department Should Undertake Research Dealing with All Aspects of the Educational Program

During the past thirty years an ever increasing number of school systems have recognized the necessity of conducting inquiries concerning the degree of efficiency which they achieve. A recent publication of the United States Office of Education lists more than 100 cities that have definitely organized bureaus of research. Half of these have been established since 1925.

It is even more important in the state office than it is locally that a division be set up to inquire concerning the efficiency of the schools and to conduct experiments which may result in improvements in educational practice. There is no aspect of administration, of the organization of schools, of the development of curriculums, or of the teaching process which may not be subjected to scientific inquiry.

The state office is in an advantageous position to conduct inquiries of this nature, since it has contact with all types of schools and may count on the cooperation of all professional workers in its inquiries.

Research Has Demonstrated Its Worth in Many
Fields of Work, Including Those Organized
under Private Auspices

In developing research service, education will but duplicate the experience of many other areas of human activity which have already been fundamentally transformed through replacing guess work and individual opinion by the results of scientific inquiry. The productivity of farms increased little until the establishment of scientific inquiry through the experiment stations maintained throughout the nation. An equally amazing reformation has been brought about in the practice of medicine. Only recently has medical procedure rid itself of individual guess work, opinion, and superstition. The researches of Pasteur and those who have followed in his footsteps have resulted in procedures in the practice of medicine and surgery which have added many years to the average life of man. Industry has been remade by scientific research. New facts about the properties of raw materials, new machines which improve the efficiency of production lie at the very foundation of industrial progress.

[96]

Researches Already Made in Education Have More
Than Justified the Expenditures Involved

Education has made considerable progress in this direction in recent years. The research in the psychology of learning has already brought results that are worth all of the money spent in all educational research. Children who were handicapped and for whom there seemed little hope for achievement have been given that remedial treatment which has enabled them to succeed in their school work. Other studies that have analyzed the learning process have added greatly to the speed and ease with which children acquire the tools with which all educated persons must work.

In many other fields significant results have been attained. No one acquainted with the literature of educational finance would deny the importance of the contribution that has been made in this area. It is possible from the findings of scientific inquiries in this field to propose methods for the financing of the schools that will achieve results in equalizing opportunity and in an equitable distribution of the burden of support that were unknown a generation ago.

The curriculums of the elementary and secondary schools have been almost completely remade during the past fifteen years, on the basis of researches undertaken in curriculum departments in city and state offices of education and in university schools of education. Much that was obsolete has been abandoned; reorganization around major centers of life interest has been substituted for the rigid subject matter classifications which once prevailed. Even where this major reorganization

[97]

has not yet taken place, the curriculums developed on the basis of scientific inquiry have presented to students major classifications of experience which lend themselves to more meaningful learning. In like manner, inquiries having to do with the classification and progress of children in the schools, with the preparation of efficient professional workers for the schools, and the like, have modified educational practice in the direction of greater efficiency and economy. Many fields of scientific inquiry will yield their most significant results only when instituted over a relatively wide area. For this reason research may be thought of as the most significant function of a state department of education.

State School Administration Offers
Great Opportunities for Leadership

The history of American education records the great contribution made to the stimulation of local endeavor through the leadership of the state office. We owe the acceptance of the idea of tax-supported public schools to the leadership of such men as Horace Mann, Henry Barnard, Thaddeus Stevens, Caleb Mills, John Swett, John D. Pierce, and their successors who under most difficult circumstances carried forward the program of public education in each of the states of the Union. In later years the improvement and development of our system of elementary and secondary schools was brought to pass under the leadership of men of great devotion. They organized members of the profession and enlightened citizens in support of that universal program of education which we are about to realize in the United States. There will always be a need for men of large vision, possessing a genius for leadership, to serve our democracy in the state office of education.

CHAPTER FOUR

The Administration of Public Education: Federal Relations to Education

"This Committee believes the time has come to ordain and establish a federal headquarters for education that shall be competent to meet the increasing national responsibility for education in ways that are consistent with the policies and procedures recommended in the First Section of this report.

"To realize the policies presented in this report, there must be in the Government, close to its head coordinator, the Chief Executive, a spokesman for the American spirit and method in education, who may on all occasions express that enlightened public opinion upon educational matters which is our surest guide in formulating public policy."

—REPORT OF THE NATIONAL ADVISORY
COMMITTEE ON EDUCATION, 1931

"Individual States in most cases cannot provide adequate funds for equalization purposes. Only Federal action can provide equalization funds for interstate application. Within States, the ability of any particular State to provide funds for local equalization purposes is largely determined by whether its boundaries happen to include the industrial and commercial centers to which most of its area may be tributary. There are also definite limits to the extent to which any individual State can use taxes based upon ability to pay. These are the taxes above all others that should be used to provide funds for equalization purposes, and they can be applied effectively on a large scale only by the Federal Government."

—REPORT OF THE ADVISORY COMMITTEE
ON EDUCATION, 1938

IV

THE ADMINISTRATION OF PUBLIC EDUCATION: FEDERAL RELATIONS TO EDUCATION

NO DISCUSSION of the administration of public education would be complete without considering the relationship of the federal government to education. By the Tenth Amendment to the Constitution of the United States, "The powers not delegated to the United States by the Constitution, nor prohibited by it to the States, are reserved to the States respectively, or to the people." Since education is not mentioned in the body of the Constitution, this amendment has been interpreted as leaving to the states the complete control of their schools. On the other hand, from the very beginning of our history the federal government has provided support for public education in the several states. The justification for federal support may be found in the General Welfare Clause of the Constitution.

The Decentralized Administration of Public Education Should Be Maintained

During the first seventy-five years of our history, grants of land and of money were made to the several states in support of public education without any attempt on the part of the federal government to control or to administer the schools. Beginning with the First Morrill Act in 1862, and in subsequent legislation, the federal government exercised some degree of control

[103]

through the allocation of funds for particular phases of education. The grants for colleges of agriculture and engineering, for experiment stations, and for the extension service are examples of this type of control. The largest measure of control occurs in the Smith-Hughes Act for the support of vocational education. This measure provides for the control of courses of study, the preparation of teachers, and even the allocation of the time of students. Approval from the central authority is necessary in order to secure federal funds. There is also the provision in this case and in certain others for the matching of funds furnished by the federal government to the states. This sort of control may well mean that the state's educational program may be thrown out of balance by the desire to secure federal support.

There is need for the reconsideration of this legislation and for the repeal of those provisions which centralize in the federal government the control of education within the states.

The Experience of Other Countries Emphasizes the Desirability of Decentralized Control

In the totalitarian state education is the instrument used to regiment the thinking of the people. No longer is a search for truth encouraged. Propaganda which seeks to enlist the support of all of the people for the program of the dictator takes the place of education. Children and youth are taught that their duty lies in complete subordination of their lives and of their will to the state. Mature persons who express a belief in or exercise freedom of speech and of conscience are sent to concentration camps or are executed.

In a democratic society, particularly in our own which consists of a federation of states covering a wide geographic territory, it is important to resist any centralization of control in education. A federal system of education might, through the determination of curriculums and the presentation of class or partisan political propaganda, dominate or control the thinking of the people. A decentralized administration is a most effective means of guaranteeing freedom of speech and of discussion and of protecting the schools against the propaganda of any political group temporarily in control of the central government.

Federal Headquarters for Education Is Necessary
Even though the Administration of Schools
Is Left to the States

By Act of Congress on March 1, 1867, a Department of Education was established "for the purpose of collecting such statistics and facts as shall show the condition and progress of education in the several states and territories, and of diffusing such information respecting the organization and management of schools and school systems, and methods of teaching, as shall aid the people of the United States in the establishment and maintenance of efficient school systems, and otherwise promote the cause of education throughout the country." The Department of Education was reduced to a Bureau in the Department of the Interior a year after its creation.

As important as is the function of the national Office of Education in the collection and dissemination of information, it has other responsibilities which have necessarily increased in importance during the period of its existence. Funds must be allocated to the several states for special phases of education. The program of research already developed needs to be expanded into new areas. Experimentation may well be carried on by the federal Office in selected localities throughout the country. A good example of this type of activity is found in the experimental work being conducted in the organization of forums. Responsibility for the educational program in the Civilian Conservation Corps camps has been allocated to this Office. Experimental work is being carried on in radio education. Contacts are maintained not only with state and local public school systems but with many organized groups in the population concerned with the processes and with the product of our schools.

The Federal Education Headquarters Should
Act as a Coordinating Agency

Education is carried on by all of the departments of the federal government. Schools are maintained in outlying possessions. The education of Indians and of the Eskimos in Alaska is undertaken by the federal government. In every governmental department schools are maintained for training and up-grading personnel. While these agencies of the federal government render important service, they lack coordination. This desirable relationship cannot be brought about except upon the basis of a reorganization which would establish a more important office for education in the federal government.

The time has come to establish a federal headquarters for education, headed by an executive who is in position to cooperate with the heads of other departments of government. Three solutions of this problem have been proposed during the past ten years. The Advisory Committee reporting in 1931 recommended the establishment of a Department of Education with a Secretary in the President's Cabinet. In this Commission and in other quarters, there was extended discussion of a proposal to establish a national board or commission for education. It was argued that this competent commission, selecting its own executive without reference to party politics, would follow the American tradition of acknowledging the unique function of education in our democracy and in separating its leadership and administration from other governmental functions. A more recent proposal sought to bring about a coordination among the many agencies dealing with education in the national government by organizing a division in a Department of Public Welfare. Whatever the final disposition of the matter may be, all are agreed with respect to the necessity of establishing a more significant headquarters office for education in the national government and of providing a more adequate support for a program of research to be conducted under its auspices.

The National Interest in an Educated Citizenry Requires Greater Federal Participation in School Support

The federal government has a vital interest in the

provision of education throughout the land. We all acknowledge gladly our citizenship in the nation, in the state, and in the locality. All are concerned with the opportunity provided for individual growth and development, and with the development of an educated citizenry.

The several states vary greatly in wealth and in income. The number of children in relation to the number of adults tends to vary inversely in relation to the per capita wealth of the several states. The people of the nation move from locality to locality and from state to state as economic opportunity beckons. These and other well-established facts clearly indicate that there is little possibility of the maintenance of an adequate system of public education in our country except on the basis of a very much larger participation by the federal government in the support of the schools.

The Nation Is Becoming a Single Economic Unit

The obligation of the federal government to provide increased support is based not only upon the need of the several states but also upon the unity which exists in our economic structure. No state or locality maintains itself. Each community throughout the nation finds itself dependent upon all parts of the country. An important factor in the development of the interdependence of all sections of the country has been the financing of our economic enterprises. The production of raw materials and their manufacture and distribution are undertaken on a nation-wide basis and financed in the larger commercial centers. Incomes accruing from enterprises carried on in one part of the country are frequently subject to taxation in another area. Simple equity demands that the resources of the nation wherever they are located be taxed for the realization of the great national purpose represented in education.

The Mobility of the Population Is a
Factor of Primary Importance

An outstanding characteristic of our modern life is found in the mobility of our population. Boys and girls who go to school in rural areas may spend their adult life in cities. Large numbers of adults migrate with their families from one section of the country to another. There is no large city in the United States which has a birth rate sufficient to maintain its population. It is therefore apparent that the economic and social development of every section of the country is dependent upon the provision made for education in each of the several states.

Nothing has been more disastrous during the recent period of economic distress than has been the denial of educational opportunity to American boys and girls. Nothing can more certainly make for the strength and economic security of our people in the years which lie ahead than the provision of an adequate program of education throughout the nation.

Larger Federal Support Is Necessary

There are states in the Union that cannot support an adequate system of public education. Even if a model

[109]

tax system were to be developed in certain of the poorer states, the money accruing therefrom would not be sufficient to maintain a reasonably adequate program of education for all the children and youth within their borders. It is a fact that, in general, the poorer states now make greater effort in support of education as represented by the tax burden which they bear in relation to their economic resources than do the wealthier states. It has also been established that the number of adults in the population in relation to the number of children of school age varies greatly among the several states and that the higher ratios of school population to the supporting adult population are found in the poorer states.[1] Because of these facts and because of the inequities involved in the tax structure as between the state and federal government and as among the several states, larger federal support must be provided.

Federal Support Can Be Granted without Federal Control

Attention has already been called to the fact that a large measure of federal support was granted to public education during the first seventy-five years of our national history without federal control of schools. The danger of federal control must be recognized. It is possible, however, to draft financial legislation, as has been done in recent years, providing definitely for the maintenance of state and local control in the adminis-

---

[1] Educational Policies Commission, National Education Association and American Association of School Administrators. *The Effect of Population Changes on American Education*. Washington: the Commission, 1938. 58 p. Price, 50c.

tration of schools, in the determination of curriculums and courses of study, and in the processes of education as carried on in the classroom. A wise recommendation in the Report of the President's Advisory Committee on Education proposes that those sections of the Smith-Hughes law which give authority to the federal government be repealed. There is no reason why the doctrine should be accepted that the distribution of federal money to the states necessarily carries with it the control of education by the central government.

Federal Control Has Been Exercised by Various Means

The issue of federal control needs to be fully explored. In rare instances federal legislation has definitely provided for control by a federal agency. This is particularly true in the case of the Smith-Hughes law, providing for the development of a program of vocational education. In Section 11 of this law will be found the following statement of requirements which must be met by the state:

". . . that such schools or classes giving instruction to persons who have not entered upon employment shall require that at least half of the time of such instruction be given to practical work on a useful or productive basis, such instruction to extend over not less than nine months per year and not less than thirty hours per week; that at least one-third of the sum appropriated to any State for the salaries of teachers of trade, home economics, and industrial subjects shall, if expended, be applied to part-time schools or classes for workers over fourteen

[111]

years of age who have entered upon employment, and such subjects in a part-time school or class may mean any subject given to enlarge the civic or vocational intelligence of such workers over fourteen and less than eighteen years of age; that such part-time schools or classes shall provide for not less than one hundred and forty-four hours of classroom instruction per year; that evening industrial schools shall fix the age of sixteen years as a minimum entrance requirement and shall confine instruction to that which is supplemental to the daily employment; that the teachers of any trade or industrial subject in any State shall have at least the minimum qualifications for teachers of such subject determined upon for such State by the State board, with the approval of the Federal Board for Vocational Education. . . ." (39 Stat. 934.)

These and other provisions of this law provided for direct control of curriculums, the organization of schools, and the qualifications of teachers. This is a clear example of specific legislation which places control in the federal government.

In the Smith-Hughes law, and in certain others dealing with the programs of vocational education, the matching by the state of the moneys distributed to them by the federal government is required. This is an insidious type of control. It is quite possible that in a state money may be diverted from other phases of the educational program which very greatly need support in order that the money furnished for a special purpose by the federal government may be matched. There is no good argument in support of the plan of requiring a state to match money assigned to it by the federal government.

Still another method of control is found in the earmarking of funds for special phases of the educational program, even where matching is not required. It may well happen in a state that there is great need for support for elementary and secondary education. If the federal government earmarks money for some other purpose, then it has in some degree determined the program offered in the state and may have interfered with its sound development.

The Requirement of Submission of Plans for Educational Service within the State Should Not Be Interpreted as Giving Veto Power to any Federal Official

In many areas of government in which funds from the federal government have been made available to the states there has been a requirement that a plan for the conduct of the services supported by federal appropriations be submitted by the state authority to federal officials as a preliminary step before funds are allocated. Such provisions as are at present operating seem to have resulted primarily in encouraging state officials to maintain a high standard of service and in acquainting them with good practices as carried on in other states and as proposed by the federal authority.

So long as the requirement of the submission of plans results in effecting the purpose of the federal grant and does not lead to control in the organization of schools, in the determination of curriculums, or in the processes of education, nothing but good can result. It is essential, however, that members of the profession exercise eternal vigilance to the end that the submission of plans shall not lead to rigid uniformity throughout the nation, shall not require the approval by federal authorities less well acquainted with the needs of the state than are the persons submitting the plans, and that the federal authority shall not have the right to veto state plans.

Another form of control is that involved in grants for emergency purposes. Wherever moneys are made available on this basis, some federal officer must determine whether or not an emergency exists. There is grave danger, wherever discretion is given to a governmental officer, that pressures which he may be unable to resist will be brought to bear upon him and that the net result will be the distribution of money on the basis of political patronage.

The Federal Government May Wisely Continue Support of Those Phases of Education Already Subsidized, and Should Encourage Experimentation

Ideally and in the long run federal support for education should be provided for the purpose of encouraging all types of public education within the states. In the light of our current practice it is desirable that moneys already allocated by the federal government and earmarked for particular phases of education be continued until the support of education by the federal government and by the states is sufficient to enable the states to include in their general support of education those services now specifically subsidized.

The federal government should, as well, share responsibility with the states and localities for the stimulation of new types of education and their demonstration in selected centers throughout the country. A good example of this form of experimentation is found in the support by the federal government of forums in which adults participate in the discussion of current problems. Sound policy supports this procedure with the understanding that once the experiment has been made and its success determined, then special earmarking of federal money for forums or other new types of educational activity should be discontinued.

The Federal Government May Audit the Funds It Distributes without Controlling the Schools

In distributing funds to the states, good practice demands that the federal government check against the expenditures made in order to determine that the funds have been used for the purposes for which they are appropriated. An audit by an officer of the federal government designed to determine that moneys appropriated for education have been expended within the state for this purpose, need in no way interfere with the management or control of education or the choice of educational means, processes, and programs carried on by the state and local governments.

Federal Money Should Be Distributed on an Objective Basis

Legislation having to do with federal support should be based upon scientifically determined measures. There are already available a considerable body of tested experience in the apportionment of state support for education, and much evidence dealing with the needs and abilities of the several states to support a system of public education. Appropriations determined by the needs of the several states in relation to their ability to support education should be turned over to the states without specifying the particular phase or phases of public education to be supported from these funds.

The Maintenance of Our Democracy Is Dependent upon the Education of All of Its Citizens

The teaching profession has a solemn obligation to bring to the attention of all of our citizens and to enlist their cooperation in the improvement of the program of public education throughout the nation. If our democracy is to persist, it must be upon the basis of an intelligent consideration of common problems by all the people. The ideal of democracy demands that all of us sacrifice in order that we may make our contribution to the common good. Whatever disaster may for the time being interfere with our economic well-being, nothing can in the long run prevail against a society which is made up of citizens who work and live sympathetically, intelligently, and cooperatively.

CHAPTER FIVE

Public Schools

"Congress shall make no law respecting an establishment of religion, or prohibiting the free exercise thereof; or abridging the freedom of speech, or of the press; or the right of the people peaceably to assemble, and to petition the Government for a redress of grievances."

—Article I, AMENDMENTS TO THE
CONSTITUTION OF THE UNITED STATES

"In one field the state would seem at first sight to usurp the family function, the field, namely, of education. But such is not in reality the case. Education is the proper office of the state for two reasons, both of which come within the principles we have been discussing. Popular education is necessary for the preservation of those conditions of freedom, political and social, which are indispensable to free individual development. And, in the second place, no instrumentality less universal in its power and authority than government can secure popular education."

—WOODROW WILSON, THE STATE

"Neither the state nor any subdivision thereof, shall use its property or credit or any public money, or authorize or permit either to be used, directly or indirectly, in aid or maintenance, other than for examination or inspection, of any school or institution of learning wholly or in part under the control or direction of any religious denomination, or in which any denominational tenet or doctrine is taught."

—NEW YORK STATE CONSTITUTION,
Article 9, Section 4

V

Public Schools

THE discussion of policy in the preceding chapters has been concerned almost exclusively with issues affecting the tax-supported system of public education. If one were to discuss the problems of the curriculums offered, the organization of schools and classes, and the development of a complete school system under private auspices, his conclusions for the most part would follow those which have been set down as applying in the field of public education. The major distinctions that would have to be made would concern the purposes, financing, and control of these schools.

Education Is a Function of the State

From the days of the founding fathers down to the present time education has been acknowledged as necessary for the preservation of our democracy. As the need for this service came to be recognized, tax-supported and publicly controlled schools were established. Other schools, organized and administered under private auspices, have been maintained with the distinct understanding that the instruction offered in them conforms in general to the program which the state requires for all its citizens.

The Purposes of Many Non-Public Schools Are
Not Those Which We Seek through Our
System of Public Education

Schools which are supported and controlled by private bodies may seek the same ends as those which actuate public institutions. Many of the universities organized on private foundations are in a very real sense public institutions. They may provide opportunities that parallel and in many cases exceed the opportunities for liberal training, for professional education, or for research offered in publicly controlled and tax-supported institutions. By far the greater number of schools on the elementary and secondary level, organized and maintained under private auspices, seek to realize purposes not contemplated by our system of public education. They seek to teach some particular religious or political belief or dogma. They may be organized with the idea of segregating children whose parents believe that their education is best secured in association with those of their own economic and social group. The presence of these schools serving a special purpose cannot fail to divert the interest of citizens in the maintenance and improvement of a system of public education. If children are sent to private schools because public schools, in the opinion of their parents, are not good enough, then one may not always expect these same parents to work diligently for the improvement of the public school system. If children are sent to schools in order that they may be kept under the influence of a particular religious belief then their parents inevitably feel the double burden of supporting the private school which their children attend, while paying taxation in support of public schools. No one would deny to the parents the acceptance of their obligation to provide religious education for their children. Most of our citizens would urge that this education be provided by the home and by the church while leaving to the public school system the provision of secular education. If we acknowledge that education is a function of the state then we should seek to develop a public school system good enough for all and adequate to meet the needs of all of our citizens.

Public Schools Must Be Secular Schools

One of the great achievements of our democracy has been the establishment of freedom of religious belief. The First Amendment to the Constitution provides that "Congress shall make no law respecting an establishment of religion, or prohibiting the free exercise thereof." This same guarantee will be found in the constitutions of all the states. There is a distinct prohibition against the compulsory support of religion through taxation. There is no restraint upon the holding of particular religious beliefs or their expression. The ideal of complete religious freedom necessarily involves the secularization of tax-supported schools. No doctrine can be taught that may not violate the belief or conscience of some pupil attending the school or of his parents. Even the reading of the Bible and the reciting of the Lord's Prayer as a daily exercise in the schools is properly interpreted as opposed to the guarantee of religious freedom. Any type of religious instruction in public schools may be interpreted by the taxpayer as the enforced support of the particular religious doctrine that is presented.

The Separation of Church and State
Permits Freedom of Action by Each
in Its Own Sphere

The complete separation of church and state leaves all religious groups—Protestant, Catholic, Jewish, or any other—free to conduct worship, to instruct children, and to express the beliefs which they hold sacred. The Supreme Court of the United States has held unconstitutional a legislative enactment which sought to compel all children to attend public schools.

Any church group has the right to organize schools in which its particular doctrine is taught, provided only that since these schools are organized to take the place of public education, their curriculums must include those experiences deemed necessary for the preparation of all for citizenship. On the other hand, this same freedom denies to any religious body support derived from the taxation of all the people. Constitutions, court decisions, and legislative enactments definitely point to the same conclusion, namely, that religious liberty can be maintained only on the basis of complete separation of church and state. This political doctrine should not be interpreted as anti-religious. Those who adhere most firmly to it recognize the desirability of providing religious education in homes and in churches.

State Constitutions Prohibit Use of Public Money
for Private or Parochial Schools

The states of the Union typically provide, either by the constitutions or by the interpretation of the courts, that public money should not be allotted to private or sectarian schools. If these provisions were to be modified and money were to be made available to schools controlled and administered by private individuals or by religious bodies, the principle of the separation of church and state would be violated. Such action would lead inevitably to a situation in which each denominational group would seek support for its own school, and the people's public schools would inevitably disappear as an important agency of government.

Those who advocate the distribution of public money to private and sectarian schools may well consider the problem of control which will inevitably arise should such action be taken. If the state furnishes support it is under the obligation to inquire concerning the program of instruction offered and to require a strict accounting of the moneys spent. In the great majority of our local communities throughout the nation the delegation of these responsibilities to local boards of education would lead to conflict between the public authority and those responsible for the non-public school. While some advantage might seem to accrue to the non-public school temporarily, in the long run the breakdown in the principle of the separation of church and state by the diversion of public money to the support of privately controlled schools will lead directly into the controversy and bitterness which has characterized the struggle for the secularization of education in other countries.

There Is a Movement to Use Public Money for Services to Children Not Attending Publicly Controlled Schools

A campaign for the allocation of public money to private and sectarian schools has been vigorously supported in recent years. It is argued that non-public schools render an important service to the state. It is proposed that an equitable distribution be made of the tax money collected between the public school system and schools maintained under private auspices. Legislation has been sought that would carry into effect this diversion of public funds to the support of non-public schools. Movements are under way to revise the constitutions of the several states to remove the prohibition against the use of public money in this manner. Those who believe in the establishment of a universal system of public education and in the maintenance of the doctrine of the separation of the church and the state will find it necessary to resist this movement vigorously and openly. It will be necessary to be on guard against measures of doubtful validity which seem innocent enough in themselves but which offer an entering wedge which will result in the long run in the abandonment of the fundamental principle to which we are committed.

There Are Services Which the State Should Offer to All Children

The enforcement of compulsory education is a function of the state. When children are enrolled in private or parochial schools, the state is just as certainly interested in their regular attendance as it is in the attendance of the children attending public schools. There is no direct support for private and parochial schools involved in enforcing the compulsory education law.

Health services, including health examinations and the control of contagious diseases, are measures taken for the protection of all children in the community. These services may well be made available for all boys and girls regardless of the schools which they attend. The protection of the health of children may not be construed as a subsidy to the school in which they are enrolled.

The Struggle To Preserve the Separation of Church and State Will Be Fought Out in Each of the Several States

The First Amendment to the Constitution of the United States, already referred to, makes provision against the allocation of money from the federal government to sectarian schools. As has been noted, the Constitutional provisions in each of the several states operate to maintain the same principle. But constitutions can be changed and the courts may modify their interpretations of Constitutional provisions. The maintenance of the doctrine of the separation of church and state is of greater importance to the American people than is the distribution of federal money in support of schools in the several states.

The Public Schools Are the One Institution Set Up
for the Purpose of Developing Social
Solidarity in the Whole Population

If American democracy is to succeed, it must be on the basis of the sympathy and understanding existing among all groups whatever their racial extraction or religious affiliation. The public school is the place in which all of the children of all of the people, without regard to religious affiliation of their parents, may work together. Good administration seeks to make certain that nothing in the practices of the schools shall set one group against another or distinguish among those who are there receiving that tuition which will prepare them for citizenship in their common country. In the publicly controlled and publicly supported institutions there can be developed good will, tolerance, and the practice of cooperation among all the people. The public schools are the foundation upon which democracy is built.

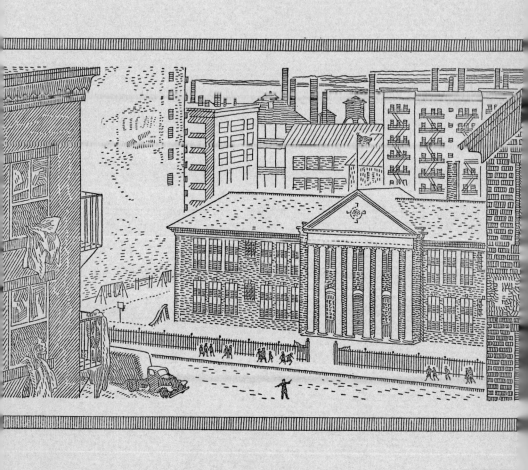